# Musical
# Involvement

# Musical Involvement

## A Guide to Perceptive Listening

**DONALD J. FUNES**
*State University of New York
College at Potsdam*

**KENNETH MUNSON**
*St. Lawrence University*

Harcourt Brace Jovanovich, Inc.
*New York   Chicago   San Francisco   Atlanta*

The cover painting: *Les Musiciens* by Graciela Rodo Boulanger.
© by the artist. All rights reserved.

ISBN: 0-15-564950-7

Library of Congress Catalog Card Number: 74-25016

Printed in the United States of America

*Illustration Credits*

Introduction: page 2, Lynda Gordon; 3, Clyde Hare, courtesy Cities Service Company; 5, Collection, Museum of Modern Art, New York, purchase. Oil on canvas, 75⅞" x 58". Chapter 1: page 8, courtesy Performing Artservices, New York; photo, David B. Miller; 9, reprinted with permission from *The Drama Review*, vol. 14, no. 1 (T-45), Fall 1969, © 1969. All rights reserved; 14–15, Marjorie Pickens; 18, courtesy Performing Artservices, New York; 20, Ken Haas for Music-One; 23, © Gabriel D. Hackett. Chapter 2: page 26, courtesy Joslyn Art Museum, Omaha; 28 (top), Collection, Museum of Modern Art, New York. Oil on canvas, 50" x 50"; 28 (bottom), Collection, Alfonso A. Ossorio and Edward F. Dragon, East Hampton, N.Y.; 32, courtesy Wesleyan University, Middletown, Conn. Chapter 3: page 40, George Holton, Photo Researchers, Inc.; 44, courtesy Consulate General of India; 47, Russ Kinne, Photo Researchers, Inc. Chapter 4: page 56, courtesy Museum of Fine Arts, Boston, M. and M. Karolik Collection. Pen and water color, 18" x 23⅞"; 61 (top left), courtesy British Museum; 61 (top right), Butler Institute of American Art, Youngstown, Ohio. Oil, 32" x 40"; 61 (bottom), courtesy Leo Castelli Gallery, New York. Collection of the artist. Oil on canvas, 72" x 54"; 65, courtesy French Embassy, Press and Information Division, New York. Chapter 5: page 68, Dr. Hugh Linebach. © 1968, 1972 by Harcourt Brace Jovanovich, Inc.; from *Psychology: An Introduction*, 2nd ed., by Jerome Kagan and Ernest Havemann; 79, Alinari, Art Reference Bureau; 83, Brown Brothers. Chapter 6: page 90, courtesy Consulate General of Japan, New York; 91, Scala; 93, courtesy Henry Francis du Pont Winterthur Museum, Winterthur, Del.; 96, Metropolitan Museum of Art, New York. Gift of Alexander Smith Cochran, 1913; 98, Museum of Modern Art, New York. Acquired through the Lillie P. Bliss Bequest. Oil on canvas, 29" x 36¼". Chapter 7: page 108 (top left and right), Lynda Gordon. Collection, Museum of Modern Art, New York. A. Conger Goodyear Fund. Bronze (cast 1950), 59¼" x 46½"; at base 45" x 29⅞"; 108 (bottom), photo, Museum of Modern Art, New York; 117, Metropolitan Museum of Art, Harris Brisbane Dick Fund, 1939; 118, photo courtesy Victor Vasarely; 195 x 130 cm.; 124, courtesy Escher Foundation, Haags Gemeentemuseum, The Hague. Woodcut, 44 x 44 cm. Chapter 8: page 131, courtesy Staempfli Gallery, New York; 135, National Gallery of Art, Washington, D.C. Gift of Edgar William and Bernice Chrysler Garbisch; 142, wedding quilt, formerly in the collection of Mrs. Clarence C. Wells. Pieced appliqué and embroidery, cotton, approx. 80" x 80"; 144, gravestone of the Holmes children, East Glastonbury, Conn. Photo by Ann Parker. Photos on 142 and 144 © 1974 The Whitney Museum of American Art; both are from *The Flowering of American Folk Art 1776–1876* by Jean Lipman and Alice Winchester. Chapter 9: page 152, Myron Woods, Photo Researchers, Inc.; 157, David Berlin, Chimera Foundation, Inc. © *Dance Perspectives 48*; 161, Memorial Art Gallery of the University of Rochester, Marion Stratton Gould Fund. Oil on canvas, 40" x 32"; 162–63, courtesy Kazuko Hillyer International.

# Preface

This brief introduction to music, designed for quarter or semester courses, presupposes no musical training of any kind. The only prerequisite for its use is the willingness to become an activist in listening to music and in creating musical experiences, with students and instructor together pursuing the goal of musical perceptiveness through musical involvement.

The book does not divide music into categories—"good" or "bad," "popular" or "classical," "ours" or "theirs"—and it does not describe traditional styles or retell music history. What the book does do is reach out toward the music of all cultures and times, taking in music of Africa and Asia along with western folk music, rock, jazz, the standard concert repertory, and the frontiers of composition today. All these are explored for the features they share: sound, time, rhythm, pitch, and the orderly effects of growth and structure. Running through the step-by-step focus on each of these elements is the unifying concept of tension-and-repose cycles. In comment and example, each element is probed in terms of these ever recurring cycles that are central to whatever impact music makes on us.

Throughout the book, two principal devices frame the students' activist role:

1. Questions to be answered. Concentrated listening is required to answer these direct questions about a specific musical event at a given moment in a particular piece. The answers—often simple and always brief—are supplied at the end of the book, allowing students the reward of point-by-point discovery.

2. Independent projects. A variety of individual and group projects invite creative participation in composing and performing at whatever level each student can command. All the projects reinforce some particular concept, and all are designed to enhance listening by doing.

In addition, many of the photographs encourage students to reach beyond music in an active exploration of parallels in the other arts. By all these means, this book and its 180 recorded musical illustrations aim to aid the development of that full involvement which alone provides the ultimate rewards of listening.

The stance and substance of this book come out of the crucible of the 1960s. In particular personal ways, they were affected by Robert Trotter of the University of Oregon and by Jane M. Saunders. In broader terms they were shaped by the musical life and times of our students and by the seminal ideas of John Cage, Leonard Meyer, and Marshall McLuhan. We owe a great deal to the vision and faith of Nina Gunzenhauser of Harcourt Brace Jovanovich, and we acknowledge our special debt to our editor, Natalie Bowen, whose sure hand and sharp editorial skills guided the later stages of our labor. Our thanks go to John F. Park of Ulster County Community College and R. Scott Stringham of West Virginia University for their helpful comments, and to David Berry, Gail Berry, Earle Brown, Cynthia Dybdahl, F. Eugene Dybdahl, and Paul Roland for performing pieces we could not have included without their help. Finally, a large measure of gratitude goes to the Funes family, who staunchly withstood this prolonged siege of bookmaking.

D. J. F.
K. M.

# Contents

# Introduction

Hearing music and responding to it actively is *listening*, something
very different from merely basking in agreeable sounds. This
book will help you learn to listen—to heighten your musical awareness, develop a number of listening skills, and involve yourself
in music old and new, music of the Americas, Africa, Asia, and
Europe.

## The Aesthetic Attitude

Listening to music involves a particular attitude, the aesthetic
attitude. To perceive music (or anything else) aesthetically, you
need to be able to "distance" yourself from it—to filter out and set
aside all the personal associations and practical considerations you
bring to your other experiences. To the degree that you can do
this, you are perceiving aesthetically: you are perceiving an object,
an experience, or a work of art for its own sake.

As an example of distancing, think of a peaceful country scene—a meadow with cattle grazing beside a stream, a stand of pine trees nearby. To a real estate developer the scene might represent six acres ripe for subdivision and profit. A scientist might see there the raw materials for ecological or geological data. A passing driver might be looking for the stream as a landmark in a set of directions. A fisherman's eyes might light up at the possibility of trout for lunch, while the farmer-owner would probably be thinking in economic terms—the health of the cattle, the condition of the alfalfa, the lumber potential of the trees. These perceptions differ, but they are all *practical*: the scene is taken in not for what it is, but as a means to some end. Though all these people might be partly free from ulterior motives, the best chance for aesthetic perception might be that of a hiker, who has no purpose other than to see, hear, smell, and enjoy. His or her experience is utterly *impractical*, an end in itself.

*The impractical eye can find beauty anywhere—in the middle of a city street, for example, or in the cooling tower of a natural gas plant (opposite).*

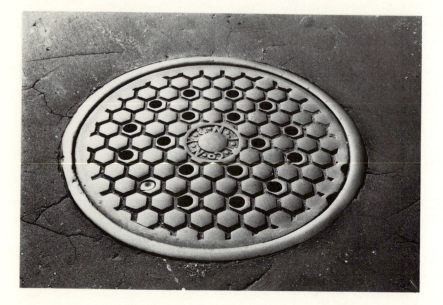

Walk slowly to class and try to *notice*. Listen, look, and touch.

Try to fit each of the following objects or situations into one of these five categories: biological, intellectual, moral-religious, economic, and aesthetic. You may find that some will fit into more than one category, depending on your attitude.

a bird call
a foot race
hand lotion
an advertisement showing a beautiful girl in a bikini
a line of people in a bank
a test tube

There are two common reasons why the distancing necessary for aesthetic perception may be hard for you to achieve when you listen to music. One is the habit we all have at times of letting a piece evoke highly personal memories, images, and fantasies; these can be very pleasant, but they have nothing to do with experiencing a piece of music as a thing-in-itself. The other reason is the specific connotation a piece may take on because of its identification with a particular film or television program. If you have seen the movie *2001*, for instance, you will almost certainly have a great deal of forgetting to do if you want to hear the following example in a strictly musical way. Once they are present, visual connotations are difficult to unload.

Example     Richard Strauss
                 *Thus Spake Zarathustra* (excerpt), 1896

Besides distancing, another condition necessary for aesthetic perception is *sympathetic awareness,* which means an openness on your part—a willingness to set aside any prejudices, so that you do not reject a piece of music before you have confronted it fully. It means that you will enter into any musical experience on its own terms, seeking out its individuality rather than expecting what it does not promise. To reject a Beethoven symphony because it is different from a Rolling Stones song—or vice versa—is as counter-productive as asking for a skirt on Botticelli's Venus.

When you accept these conditions for pursuing the full possibilities of musical experience, you will inevitably refine your perception. Without any help, you would doubtless do this intuitively with much listening over a long period. But with the assistance of this book, you should be able to speed up the process, because the book will help you organize what your ear takes in so that you will notice relationships you might otherwise miss. It may also help you increase your awareness of relationships in the other arts, for in the long run, the attitudes and the modes of perception you develop in listening to music will be useful to you in confronting *all* aesthetic experiences.

*Have you any difficulty in confronting this painting fully? Can you summon enough sympathetic awareness to try to discern and appreciate the artist's purpose? (Woman I, 1952, by Willem de Kooning)*

Find five things not usually considered works of art and describe their "aesthetic" qualities.

Try to find three things that can't be described in aesthetic terms.

Listen to three pieces of music you have never liked, trying to determine why you have been unsympathetic toward them. Now listen again, trying to see if they have any characteristics worth the effort of aesthetic perception.

Choose a piece of music with your instructor and the other members of your class. With them, try to distance yourself, and describe only those features that are relevant to aesthetic perception.

# 1 *Our Sound Environment*

Which is more musical:
    the sound of breaking glass or the sound of a violin?
    the sound of a siren or the sound of an oboe?
    the "sound" of silence or the sound of a C chord?
What is music?

A decade ago the answers to these questions would have seemed self-evident to nearly everyone. Not today. Television and modern technology have engulfed music in a sound explosion—sounds from every culture, sounds from within the earth, sounds from the ocean floor, sounds from outer space. The narrow limits of traditional western European music-making have been increasingly challenged by composers who choose their sound material from the total environment, unwilling to be bound by only those sounds that musical custom has consecrated.

There is little profit in arguing what is and what is not music. Unarguably, music does involve sound and time; when these two elements are organized in some way, music results. (Or is music simply the *existence* of sound in time?) Organization implies patterns of relationship, some of which we will be exploring in this book. For the moment, though, try responding to sound *as sound* in a small sampler of the rich sound environment employed in music-making today.

## Electronic Resources

It hardly seems an overstatement to say that the microphone, amplifier, speaker, tape recorder, and synthesizer are the most significant musical resources of the twentieth century. They create, transform, and disseminate sound in ways that affect our entire musical experience.

*Mother Mallard's Portable Masterpiece Company, a contemporary ensemble, with a battery of electronic instruments and equipment. Left, an electronic piano; middle, a two-keyboard Moog synthesizer; right, a mini-Moog.*

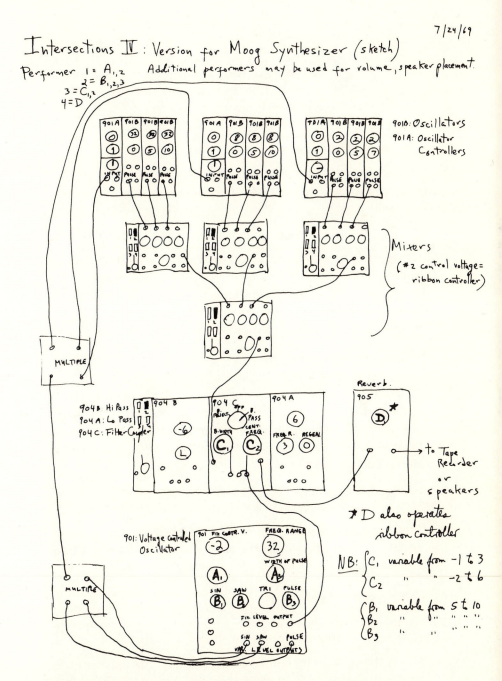

A sketch of the components of a Moog synthesizer,
showing the connections for a performance of
Intersections IV by Paul Epstein.

Example **1.1**   John McLaughlin
*Dream* (excerpt), 1973

Electric guitars, the staple of rock groups, are probably the most familiar new sound sources made possible by electronics. Here, a violin is electrified as well.

Example **1.2**   Earle Brown
*Four Systems* (excerpt), 1964

In this piece the possibilities of four conventional cymbals are greatly extended by electronic manipulation.

Example **1.3**   Luciano Berio
*Theme: Homage to James Joyce* (excerpt), 1967

This work demonstrates how extensively the sound of a human voice can be modified by a tape recorder. The original Joyce text (from Molly Bloom's soliloquy at the end of *Ulysses*) is slowed down, speeded up, spliced into new orders, played in reverse, put through filters, and overdubbed.

Example **1.4**   Ilhan Mimaroglu
*Intermezzo* (excerpt), 1965

This is an example of music created by a synthesizer in an electronic music studio. Most of the sounds were generated electronically and modified by a number of devices. Stored on different tapes, the sounds were mixed down to a two-channel stereo end product.

Example **1.5**   Jon Appleton
*Times Square Times Ten* (excerpt), 1969

This piece combines actual environmental sounds from New York City, electronically synthesized sounds, and other sounds that have been collected, mixed down, and recorded.

## Multisensory Experience

Example **1.6**   Mark Riener
*Phlegethon* (excerpt), 1970

This is the sound element of a "happening" that involves the senses of seeing and smelling as well as the sense of hearing.

Presenting only the ear's part obviously robs the work of much
of its effect. The sounds are those created by burning plastic
wrap as it drips into aluminum trays filled with water. The wrap
is draped over several coat hangers, positioned above different
parts of the stage to simulate chandeliers. Each "chandelier"
is lit at a different time, and, as the material burns, ascending
sounds result. The audience hears the sounds, smells the odor,
and sees the glow, color, and smoke generated. Because of
the latter, the composer suggests performance just before
intermission or at the end of the concert!

Experiment with objects not normally considered musical instruments and try to create interesting sounds. Create short sound
pieces using natural objects such as stones and sticks, and small
machines such as hair driers or egg beaters.

Discuss the sources of music. What stimulates the act of composing?

## Traditional Resources: Sounds New and Old

For over two hundred years music of the European-American
culture has been written for a sizable number of string, wind,
percussion, and keyboard instruments in a large variety of combinations. If there are any instruments whose sounds are unfamiliar to
you, you may want to listen to one of the several recordings cur-
rently available that demonstrate each instrument in some depth.
No matter how familiar you are, or become, with these traditional
sound sources, you are likely to encounter some surprises in the
nontraditional uses to which they are put in some of the following
examples.

### STRINGS

Violins, violas, cellos, and contrabasses (also called simply *basses*)
together make up the largest part of the traditional symphony
orchestra. These instruments, normally bowed, may also be plucked
or struck; they are flexible enough to produce a wide range of
different sounds.

Example **1.7**    Krzysztof Penderecki
*Threnody: To the Victims of Hiroshima* (excerpt), 1960

Penderecki's sound source is a fifty-two-piece string orchestra
of violins, violas, cellos, and basses. You will hear a great
variety of sound effects, among them knuckles tapping on the
instruments; strings and the instruments themselves being hit
with bows; and fingers sliding up and down strings while
the strings are being bowed. Many of the sounds seem to take
on human qualities. This threnody, or hymn of sorrow, was
written to commemorate the victims of the first atomic bomb
attack.

Example **1.8**    Peter Ilich Tchaikovsky
*Serenade for Strings,* finale (excerpt), 1880

The extraordinary contrast between this work and the Penderecki points up the striking increase in the range of demands
on the instruments since the late nineteenth century. Within
a more conservative idiom, however, Tchaikovsky achieves a
variety of effects. The excerpt begins with the strings muted, so
that the amount of vibration transmitted to the body of the
instrument is lessened and the sound somewhat muffled.
Following a short silence, as the piece moves to a faster
section, the mutes are removed. Toward the end of the excerpt
some of the strings are played pizzicato (plucked) while the rest
are bowed.

Other strings, such as guitars and banjos, are doubtless well known
to you. They too are capable of many kinds of sound that you
may want to explore.

WINDS

There are two families of instruments in which sound is initiated by
the performer's breath: "woodwinds" and brasses. In the former
(some of which are made of metal, rubber, or plastic) the air column inside the instrument is made to vibrate by:

blowing across a hole (flutes of various sizes)
blowing against a single reed (clarinets, saxophones)
blowing against a double reed (oboe, English horn, bassoon)

Example **1.9**   Elliott Carter
                  *Eight Etudes and a Fantasy*, Etude No. 6, 1950

This excerpt opens with the bassoon, followed by clarinet,
flute, and later, oboe. In addition to flutter-tonguing (a very
rapid rolling of the tongue of the kind used to say "brrr"), the
other special effects heard are the fast alternations of pitches
known as trills and tremolos.

Example **1.10**   Giacomo Rossini
                   *Wind Quartet No. 4,* third movement (excerpt), c. 1835

This work uses one brass instrument, the French horn, which
is a frequent member of wind ensembles. The other instruments
are the clarinet, flute, and bassoon. All are treated in much
more conventional ways than in Example 1.9.

BRASSES

Brass instruments—trumpet, French horn, trombone, and tuba—all
use the vibration of the player's lips to set the instrument's air
column in motion.

Example **1.11**   Alvin Etler
                   *Sonic Sequence for Brass Quintet*, 1967

After an opening French horn solo, the horn continues,
accompanied by muted trumpet and muted trombones playing
glissando (slides moving gradually back and forth to produce
an unbroken sweep of sound). During the louder second
section, begun by trumpets with mutes off, there is a great deal
of trumpet flutter-tonguing and trombone glissando. The final
section returns to the mood of the opening, and ends with the
solo French horn, again accompanied by muted trumpet and
trombone.

*Strings. Clockwise from bottom: violins, cellos, bass, violas. (In these four photos, the players are members of the 1974 Yale Summer School Orchestra.)*

*Woodwinds. First row: a pair of flutes (left) and a pair of oboes. Second row: clarinets (left) and bassoons.*

*Brass. Left to right: French horn, trumpets, trombones, and tuba.*

*Percussion. Front: three gongs. Middle, left to right: timbales, tom-toms, bongo drums, and xylophone. Back: wood blocks (left) and marimba.*

Example **1.12**    Gregor Aichinger
            *Jubilate Deo*

Originally for voices, this sixteenth-century work demonstrates
the songlike and rhythmic capabilities of the brasses in traditional writing. Compare this piece with Example 1.11 to see once
again how much greater are the demands placed on all kinds of
instruments by many present-day composers.

PERCUSSION

The percussion family is an almost limitless array of instruments
made from wood, metal, skin, plastic, and other substances. Some
are shaken or rubbed; others are played by striking with the hand
or some other object. Until this century they have been slighted
in western European culture except for limited special effects and
narrowly defined roles.

Example **1.13**    Edgard Varèse
            *Ionisation* (excerpt), 1931

*Ionisation* was one of the first works to be written for a full
percussion ensemble, in this case twenty-four instruments.
Despite its age, it remains a very contemporary work. The two
sirens, neither percussion nor traditional, undoubtedly reflect
the composer's urban surroundings.

Example **1.14**    Franz Joseph Haydn
            *Symphony No. 100*, second movement (excerpt), 1794

The rather startling use of percussion in this quiet eighteenth-
century piece is an instance of occasional special effects in
earlier European concert music. The bass drum, cymbals, and
triangle are intended to imitate a Turkish military band, the
sound of which was a late eighteenth-century fad.

KEYBOARD INSTRUMENTS

The piano, with its single keyboard, and the organ and harpsichord, with one or more keyboards, are all played by depressing
the keys. Beyond this initial similarity, their sound is produced in

three different ways. The organ operates like a wind instrument, with each of its pipes containing an air column; the strings of the piano are struck with small hammers, while the strings of the harpsichord are plucked with a quill.

Example **1.15**    György Ligeti
*Volumina* (excerpt), 1961

Composers are still exploring the possibilities of the organ, one of the oldest surviving instruments of western music. In this work Ligeti exploits the effects of subtle changes in loudness and tone color (the characteristic sound of any voice or instrument). There is no tune or harmony in the traditional sense, only masses of ever-changing sound.

Example **1.16**    Johann Sebastian Bach
*Organ Toccata in D Minor* (excerpt), c. 1709

This piece, played on an organ built in the eighteenth century, illustrates the clean, sharp definition of melody and rhythm and some of the range of sounds characteristic of an era when organ building and organ composition were at their peak.

Since the customary sounds of the piano hardly need illustration, Examples 1.17 and 1.18 present some contemporary, nontraditional ways of exploring its resources.

Example **1.17**    Henry Cowell
*Banshee* (excerpt), c. 1910

Instead of using the keyboard, the performer leans into the piano case, scraping and striking the strings. The sound is intended to represent a banshee, a spirit in Irish folklore whose wailing foretells a death.

Example **1.18**    John Cage
*Amores*, first movement, 1943

The piano is "prepared" for performance of this piece according to instructions provided by the composer. Nuts, bolts, rubber stoppers, and other objects are wedged between the strings.

*The interior of a piano prepared by John Cage.*
*Here he has used spoons, nuts and bolts, screws,*
*and other small objects.*

Examples 1.19 and 1.20 contrast contemporary and eighteenth-century ways of using the harpsichord with works by the same two composers as in Examples 1.15 and 1.16.

Example **1.19**    György Ligeti
*Continuum* (excerpt), 1967

Example **1.20**    Johann Sebastian Bach
*Goldberg Variations*, "Aria," c. 1742

As in the case of the two organ styles, the clarity and definition of Bach's approach contrast strikingly with Ligeti's curtain of sound and the changes he creates in it.

Explore the record collection in your library. Seek out sounds you have never heard and make their acquaintance.

Experiment to see what sounds a piano can produce without the use of the keyboard.

Visit a rehearsal of one of the performing groups at your school. Listen to the characteristic sounds produced on traditional instruments. Take note of what seem to you special effects or unusual sound combinations.

## MEDIEVAL AND RENAISSANCE INSTRUMENTS

The past two or three decades have added still another dimension to our sound environment: re-creations of instruments of the more distant past in European history, together with performances that give some clue to the vast variety of instrumental tone colors in use between the thirteenth and sixteenth centuries.

Example **1.21**    Anonymous
   *I Dance in This Circle (Ich spring an diesem Ringe)*

For this fifteenth-century song the performers have chosen recorder, medieval fiddle, crumhorn (a double-reed wind instrument), transverse flute, and a percussion group of drum, tambourine, and finger cymbals.

Example **1.22**    Anonymous, *Moorish Dance (La Mourisque)*
   Claude de Sermisy, *The Injustice (Cest a grant tort)*

The first of these two sixteenth-century French pieces is played on soprano and tenor shawms (predecessors of the oboe), tenor and bass sackbuts (Renaissance trombones), and tabor (drum). In the second, the instruments are two recorders, three viols (string instruments not belonging to the violin family), two lutes and a cittern (plucked string instruments), and harpsichord.

*Members of the New York Renaissance Band with some
of their instruments. Standing, left to right: sackbut, shawm,
tabor. Seated: cornetto, bass gamba.*

## Beyond Western Culture

Marshall McLuhan, the noted Canadian media expert, maintains
that the instant communication provided by today's technology is
creating a new, single world culture. People everywhere saw Neil
Armstrong's footsteps on the moon's surface at the moment he put
them there. Wars halfway around the world have been seen live in
our living rooms, and a concert in Africa can be heard simultaneously in Iceland. This state of communications is having a profound

effect on music in the western world as the musics of other cultures break into and enrich our sound environment. The following pieces, a final sampler for this chapter, are drawn from three great cultural areas—Africa, China, and India—about which we of the West still have much to learn.

Example **1.23**   Indian music
            *Twin Conch Shell Solo* (excerpt)

One musician is playing the two conch shells simultaneously. He holds the shells to his lips, blows to vibrate the air within, and changes pitch by blowing harder, tightening his lips, or using his fingers to cover the shell openings. A most interesting aspect of this solo is the absence of any break in the sound, because of a special technique called rotary breathing, in which the player blows out air he has stored in his cheeks while replenishing his lungs by breathing in air through his nose.

Example **1.24**   Chinese music
            *Wild Geese Alighting on the Sandy Shore* (excerpt)

Two traditional Chinese instruments are heard here, the *cheng* and the *hsiao*. The *cheng* is a plucked string instrument placed horizontally before the player. It has a series of movable bridges supporting the strings; one hand alters string tension while the other plucks or strums the strings. The *hsiao* is a vertical bamboo flute.

Example **1.25**   Music of Senufo
            Xylophone orchestra

This piece, recorded in an African village in the northern part of the Ivory Coast, is full of rhythmic energy, generated by the complicated drum rhythms. The orchestra consists of four xylophones and three kettledrums. In addition, there are gourds, which act as resonators, and iron jingles, which are attached to the players' wrists.

The examples you have heard in this chapter touch on the richness and diversity of potential sound sources for music. To the time-honored sounds of traditional instruments composers will go on adding new ones as new sources are discovered or invented. And that process will never stop, for our environment and culture are continually being redefined.

## Synthesis

In this final section of each of the first seven chapters, we will present a complete small piece by way of summarizing the topic of each chapter. Sometimes, as here, we will not be able to encompass every aspect of the topic. As we have seen, our sound environment is too vast for any single piece to represent more than a small sample. With Example 1.26 we begin a process of close listening that will continue throughout the rest of the book.*

> Example **1.26**   Harry Partch
> *Barstow—8 Hitchhiker Inscriptions from a Highway
> Railing at Barstow, California*, "Number 1," 1941

Few compositions could serve as well as *Barstow* to represent our multifaceted sound environment, for it combines the fruits of a noted composer, an honored craftsman, and a modern acoustical experimenter—all in the person of Harry Partch. Drawing on cultures past and present for his models and materials, Partch built all his own instruments so that he could get the kinds of sound he wanted. You will hear four of these instruments in this work. The diamond marimba and the boo, a bamboo marimba (listen for its low snapping sounds), are both African in origin; the chromelodeon is an adaptation of the European reed organ, with Partch's own special tuning; and the surrogate kithara is based on a strummed and plucked string instrument of ancient Greece. To this eclectic combination

* From this point on, your active response in this close listening process will be sought through many questions. A few, in the discussion and in the photo captions, are meant merely to suggest a line of thought. Most, however, arise out of a particular example and call for a particular answer. These questions are labeled "Q1, Q2," etc. Listen to the sample until you feel certain of each answer; then check your answers against those supplied at the end of the book.

*Harry Partch playing the boo.*

Partch has added a text for speaker and singer taken directly from the graffiti of American hobos.

"Number 1" is divided into two parts. Part 1 begins with an instrumental introduction, followed by six lines of spoken text that are occasionally enhanced by a sung background. Part 2 is the sung portion. Here are the words of each part:

PART 1

*"Number one."*

"It's January twenty-six."

"I'm freezing."

"Ed Fitzgerald, age nineteen, five feet ten inches, black hair, brown eyes."

"Going home to Boston, Massachusetts."

"It's four p.m. and I'm hungry and broke. I wish I was dead."

"But today I am a man."

PART 2

"Going home to Boston—uh huh—Massachusetts."

"It's four p.m. and I'm hungry and broke. I wish I was dead."

"But today I am a man."

"Oh—I'm going home to Boston—uh huh—Massachusetts."

The instrumental introduction is played by the diamond marimba and the chromelodeon. The diamond marimba continues as the primary accompanying instrument throughout the spoken section.

Q1  During which line in Part 1 does the chromelodeon return?

During Part 1 the singer joins the speaker and sings "Going home . . ." several times. Each time he sings this phrase he is accompanied by the kithara and the boo. Listen to these instruments again.

Q2  How many times is the phrase "Going home . . ." interjected in Part 1?

Q3  Which two instruments are played most often during Part 2?

Q4  Which instrument is used only as a form of punctuation or emphasis in Part 2?

Q5  How many instruments are used in Part 2?

# 2 Our Time Frame

Like all the elements of music, time is more easily experienced than discussed. Every composition is a unique realization of time—not the time of the clock, in which five minutes is always 300 seconds, but the kind of psychological-experiential time in which five minutes can seem to flash by in no time or can seem to last for an eon. All music exists within this experiential time frame, but particular compositions move within it in two distinctly different ways: some music moves with an even pulse that marks off regular segments of time, while other music moves freely, with no discernible sense of pulse at all. Example 2.1 illustrates the first of these ways; Example 2.2 illustrates the second.

Example **2.1**   Joe Cocker
*Somethin' Comin' On* (excerpt), 1969

Example **2.2**   Pierre Schaeffer
*Bound Objects (Objets liés)* (excerpt), 1959

Both these types of movement in musical time have something to do with time in nature and in everyday life. The second type has some parallel in those uneven happenings—an unexpected visitor, a sudden shower, for example—that cut across the steadier rhythms

*Paintings exist in space just as music exists in time. Which is the "real" space here—the 40" × 30" of the frame or the endlessly rolling vista within it? (Stone City, Iowa, 1892, by Grant Wood)*

of nature and life's daily routines. The first type seems directly related to our ordinary activities, which we measure with agreed-upon units of time, such as seconds, minutes, days, and weeks. Though based in nature, these man-made units reflect our apparent need to regulate and keep track of where we have been and where we are going. Comparable units in all musics of the world appear to mirror the same need, suggesting some tie to our primordial roots—or even, beyond them, a link between musical time and cosmic rhythms. Whatever the case, mystical or mundane, we do respond to time in music in very active and direct ways. Whether consciously or unconsciously, we sense how time—along with other musical elements—creates the effects of tension and repose that are central to our response to music. *Tension* and *repose* are terms we will be using from now on, and you will understand more and more about their nature as we proceed.

## Pace

Pace can be defined as the rate of activity for any musical element, perceived in relation to some norm. Once a general level of activity has been established, any increase or decrease in the *rate* at which sounds change is a change of pace. In general, increasing the pace of any element tends to increase the level of tension—speeding up the pulse, making sounds louder or softer than an established level, changing the quality of sound, and so on. By the same token, decreases in the rate of any of these activities tend to lower the level of tension toward more repose. In the following examples various kinds of change of pace are present.

Example **2.3**   Franz Schubert
                 *Piano Quintet* ("Trout"), first movement (excerpt)
                 c. 1819

There are three distinct sections in this excerpt. The pace increases progressively from section to section, from the slow motion of the opening to the more rapid pace during the violin solo and the still faster pace during the piano solo. The solos themselves can be perceived as the norm, against which the increases in pace are supplied by the accompaniment.

Example **2.4**   John Coltrane
                 *A Love Supreme*, first movement (excerpt), 1964

Changes in pace here coincide with the points of greatest tension. As the solo develops, Coltrane adds more and more activity to the constant background of drums, bass, and piano, arriving at the fastest pace and the greatest tension by indirection. Pace and, with it, tension increase and decrease several times before reaching their highest point, or climax.

Q1   What happens after the climax?
Q2   Does the piece return slowly or immediately to the original pace?

Example **2.5**   Iannis Xenakis
                 *Concret P-H II*, 1958

Some smoldering charcoal and a tape recorder supply all the sounds in this piece. The charcoal sounds were recorded at differing tape speeds, were mixed, and were then rearranged

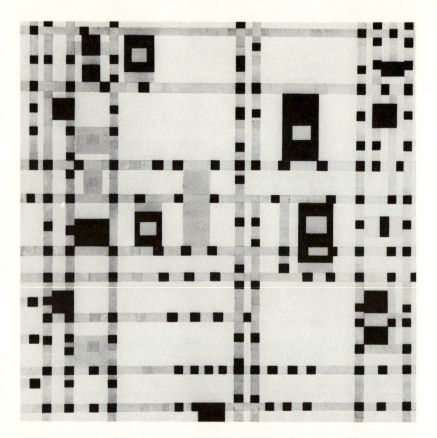

Does one of these paintings seem to you to have a greater sense of pulse than the other? And can you see a change of pace in either of them? (Above: Broadway Boogie Woogie, 1943, by Piet Mondrian; below: Lavender Mist, 1950, by Jackson Pollock)

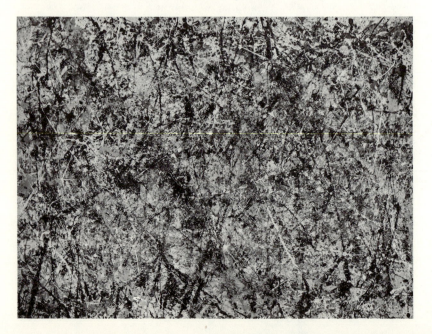

by splicing the tape. The result is a steady flow of sounds—the norm—against which changes in density (the number of events heard at one time) take place. Against this steady flow, higher and lower sounds, moving at different rates, are introduced and withdrawn.

Q3    How many times does the pace increase?
Q4    Does the pace increase or decrease at the end?

## Tempo

STEADY TEMPO

In the Xenakis piece (Example 2.5) musical events unfold in a kind of free flow, without recurring regularity. In the Coltrane (Example 2.4) we hear familiar instruments and gestures of the jazz tradition, yet the strong steady sense of pulse we expect is obscured. And because our expectations are denied, the tension level is raised. This often happens in our musical experience and in our daily experience as well. You will certainly be inclined to make a more foot-tapping response to Example 2.6 than to either the Xenakis or the Coltrane. With expectation more nearly fulfilled, the general level of tension will likely be lower.

Example **2.6**    Sonny Rollins
                        *I Got It Thad* (excerpt), 1957

In this piece, as in a great many others, you can find at least two pulse rates with which to tap along: one moderately slow, and one twice as slow as that. You will probably decide that the moderately slow rate asserts itself as the basic pulse. (Did you note a third, faster pulse rate in the saxophone part?)

The basic pulse rate defines the *tempo* of a piece. Thus, the more basic pulses there are within a given time span, the faster the tempo, and vice versa. There are no absolutes in describing tempo as fast or slow. As a rule of thumb, tempos close to a normal heart rate (72 to 76 pulses per minute) can be considered moderate;

tempos on either side are relatively slower or faster. (It is possible, of course, for a composer to indicate a tempo precisely by giving performers the specific instruction of a metronome marking: a certain note value at a certain rate per minute.)

Example **2.7**    Akira Miyoshi
*Concerto for Orchestra*, first movement (excerpt), 1964

As in the Sonny Rollins piece, you can find two pulse rates here —one very fast and one half that fast. Because nearly all parts move insistently at the very fast pulse rate, it tends to dominate and become the basic pulse, creating a very fast tempo.

CHANGES IN TEMPO

In both the preceding examples the tempo, once under way, proceeded steadily. Almost unconsciously we tend to expect this steady state as a norm in a piece of music, and thus changes in tempo intrude strongly on our awareness and tend to produce repose or tension. There are four common kinds of tempo change:

1. an abrupt shift in basic pulse rate
2. a gradual increase in basic pulse rate (*accelerando*)
3. a gradual decrease in basic pulse rate (*ritardando*)
4. a constant give-and-take in basic pulse rate (*rubato*)

We can show them graphically, like this:

| basic pulse | □ □ □ □ □ □ □ □ □ □ □ □ |
| abrupt shift | □ □ □ □  □  □  □  □ |
| accelerando | □ □ □ □ □□□□□□□□□□□□□□ |
| ritardando | □ □ □ □ □ □ □ □ □ |
| rubato | □ □□□□ □ □ □ □□□□ □ □ □ □ |

Since any change in a basic pulse rate is so easily perceived, composers and performers use tempo changes for a variety of important effects, such as signaling a new mood or the beginning or end of a musical idea. For these effects, accelerando and ritardando can help provide a smooth transition, while an abrupt tempo change tends to have a dramatic effect, heightening tension or lowering it suddenly. Speeding up or slowing down, particularly in the give-and-take of rubato, can be used to intensify the impact of a musical idea. Examples 2.8–2.12 illustrate different kinds of tempo change, sometimes more than one in a single example.

Example **2.8**    Ludwig van Beethoven
*Symphony No. 1*, first movement (opening), 1800

This excerpt has two distinct sections. The first opens with a series of sustained sounds in which it is almost impossible to sense a pulse, though the tempo is steady and the pace slow. Soon, however, the violins begin a melody with a definite pulse that confirms the slow tempo. The second section changes abruptly to a faster tempo, and the rate of activity—the pace—likewise increases.

Example **2.9**    Dmitri Shostakovich
*Symphony No. 5*, fourth movement (opening), 1937

Like Example 2.8, this excerpt has two sections. The beginning is a bold statement by brass and timpani, later punctuated by woodwinds and strings. The second section is primarily for strings.

Q5    Which of the four kinds of tempo change is used?
Q6    Does the change occur within the second section or before it?

Example **2.10**    Hector Berlioz
*Symphonie fantastique*, first movement (excerpt), 1830

There are two basic tempos, one for each of the two main sections.

Q7    Which tempo is slower, the first or second?

*A gamelan at Wesleyan University. Note the number and variety of gongs and xylophones.*

Q8   How does Berlioz change tempo from the first to the second section?

Q9   Does the change heighten the impact of the second section?

Example **2.11**    Frédéric Chopin
Nocturne, Op. 55, No. 1 (excerpt), 1844

The tempo can be determined by following the lowest pitches in the left-hand part.

Q10   Which of the four kinds of tempo change is used here?

Example **2.12**    Javanese music
Bendrong (excerpt)

This music is played by a Javanese gamelan, an orchestra consisting of bronze gongs of various sizes and metal, wood, and bamboo xylophones. After the first few sounds a steady tempo is set; the second section is in a new tempo.

Q11  Is the change in tempo from the first to the second section abrupt or gradual?

Q12  What two kinds of tempo change are used at the end of the second section? What is the reason for the first change? What is the effect of the second?

Try to find two or more performances of the Chopin nocturne in Example 2.11 and compare the interpretations. Do they all change tempo in the same places? in the same way?

See if you can find different performances of the introduction to the first movement of Beethoven's *Symphony No. 1* (Example 2.8). Compare the tempos, with the help of a metronome if possible. Which interpretation strikes you as the most effective?

Pace and tempo are two of the ways in which musical events are organized within the broad framework of time in music. Together with meter (Chapter 3) and the manipulations of meter to form patterns in time (Chapter 4), they make up *rhythm* in its broadest sense. All aspects of rhythm play a fundamental part in generating effects of tension and repose. Some of these effects have already been mentioned, and they will receive more and more attention in chapters to come.

## Synthesis

Example 2.13 will help you discover how changes in tempo and pace can interact in a complete piece. We will concentrate on these three things:

1. changes in tempo
2. changes in pace
3. differences in pace between the two voices

Example **2.13**   Giuseppi Verdi
*Rigoletto*, "Love Is the Flame" (*È il sol dell' anima*), 1851

The first part of the piece is for solo tenor voice. Here is the Italian text, with the lines numbered for easy reference:*

1. È il sol dell' anima, la vita è amore;
2. sua voce è il palpite del nostro core,
3. e fama e gloria, potenza e trono,
4. umane, fragil qui cose sono;
5. una pur avvene, sola, divina,
6. è amer che agl' angeli più ne avvincina!
7. Ah! Adunque amiamoci, donna celeste,
8. d'invidia agli uomin sarò per te,
9. d'invidia agli uomin sarò per te.

During the second part the tenor is joined by a soprano. Since the texts of the two are mixed and often repeat in fragments, the duet section will be represented graphically. Each horizontal line stands for an entrance; the line-numbering scheme is continued.

| | |
|---|---|
| 10. Soprano begins | _____  ____ |
| Tenor joins later | _____ |
| 11. Soprano continues | _____ |
| Tenor joins for conclusion | _____ |
| 12. Tenor begins | ____  _____ |
| Soprano joins | ____  ____  ____ |
| 13. Soprano begins | _____  _____ |
| Tenor joins | _____  _____ |
| 14. Together | _____ |
| 15. Vocal cadenza (passage of vocal display) together | _____ |

* Translation: "Love is the flame which fires our souls. Its voice is the beating of our hearts. Fame and glory, power and throne are but human frailties. Such joy not even angels can emulate. Ah! Love me, then, and I shall be the most envied of men."

The basic tempo of the piece is established by the orchestra at the beginning. The pace is set by the rate of change in the text. At the start, there are either one or two syllables on each pulse. The following questions will help you discover changes of tempo and pace throughout the composition.

Q13    Lines 2 and 4 have changes in tempo; they are slowed by ritardandos. What other lines of the tenor solo (lines 1–9) also have ritardandos?

Q14    Which word in line 7 is subjected to the greatest change in tempo?

Q15    In lines 2, 4, and 9, a single word (different in each line) is treated elaborately with an increase in pace. What are the three words?

Q16    Which of the lines during the tenor solo has the greatest change of pace, that is, the largest number of syllables per pulse?

Q17    Does the pace of the orchestral accompaniment increase or decrease from line 9 to line 10 (at the beginning of the soprano passage)?

Q18    Which line during the duet (lines 10–15) has the least ritardando?

Q19    Is the pace at the beginning of line 12 faster or slower than in line 11?

Q20    In lines 10–15, during which line does the soprano move at a faster pace than the tenor?

# Rhythm: Meter

## Building Blocks

METERS IN TWOS OR THREES

Like the human pulse, musical pulse is a series of undifferentiated impulses all of equal length and emphasis. But in music that has pulse (as we have seen, not all music does), we usually perceive the pulses in groups of two or three. Our sense of these groupings results from a stress or accent—real or imagined—at the start of the first pulse of each group. *Meter* is the marking of musical time by these two-pulse or three-pulse units. Thus, if you clap to the rate of your heartbeat with equal emphasis on every clap, you are simply clapping pulses, but if you clap *strong*-weak or *strong*-weak-weak you are creating two-pulse or three-pulse meters. These small units can operate separately or they can become building blocks of other, larger metrical groupings. Example 3.1 illustrates a three-pulse meter; Example 3.2 illustrates a two-pulse meter. In each example, the tempo is determined by the basic pulse rate.

Example **3.1**    Giuseppe Tartini
                   *Symphony in A Major*, third movement (excerpt), c. 1730

The tempo of the basic three-pulse group is quite fast, with the
beginning of each *strong*-weak-weak group emphasized by low
sounds in the bass:

$$| \overset{>}{\square} \; \square \; \square \; | \; \overset{>}{\square} \; \square \; \square \; |^{*}$$

* Diagrams like this one are a handy way to illustrate meter groups, and they
will be used regularly from now on. Each square represents a single pulse;
pulse groups are shown by the vertical lines; and the accented pulse is shown
by the symbol >. In multiline diagrams, the line showing the *basic pulse* is
preceded by the abbreviation BP.

Example **3.2**    John McLaughlin
                   *Resolution* (excerpt), 1972

The tempo of the basic two-pulse group is moderate. It is
partly defined by the snare drum which puts a strong accent
on the second pulse of each group; this is a simple form of
*syncopation*—the unexpected absence or displacement of the
normal first-pulse accent that defines the basic meter group.
This kind of metrical conflict is one of the most common
tension-raising devices in musical time, and we will pay more
attention to it later in this chapter. In the following diagram
the upper line shows the *strong*-weak two-pulse group with
the accent that defines it; the lower line shows the conflicting
snare drum accent.

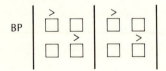

Although the meter of a piece is often described only in
terms of the basic pulse group, there are almost always pulse

groups at more than one level, sometimes at several levels simultaneously. In listening to Example 3.1, for instance, you may have
noticed a good deal of activity in the violins at a pulse rate twice as
fast as that of each basic pulse. Put another way, this faster level
of meter results from dividing each basic pulse into two parts. The
basic level and the faster level can be diagramed like this:

In *Resolution* (Example 3.2), pulse groups can be heard at four
levels, as in this diagram:

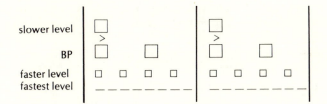

As you can see from the diagram, the pulse rate in *Resolution*
doubles at each of the faster levels. At the slower level we can sense
a grouping of each pair of basic pulses into a longer time unit
consisting of a single pulse.

Now listen to Examples 3.3–3.5. Find and tap out all the meter levels
in each, deciding first which pulse is the basic one, and then
answering the following questions for each example:

Q1   What is the tempo—fast, moderately fast, moderate, or slow?
Q2   At the basic level, are the pulses grouped by twos or threes?
Q3   At any level faster than the basic one are the pulses grouped
     by twos or threes?

*The Doge's Palace, Venice. Can you see how its pattern of arches strikingly resembles some of the diagrams in this chapter?*

Example **3.3**  Roger McGuinn and Gram Parsons
*Drug Store Truck Drivin' Man* (excerpt), 1969

Example **3.4**  Wolfgang Amadeus Mozart
*Horn Concerto No. 4*, K. 495
third movement (excerpt), 1786

Example **3.5**  Scott Joplin
*Maple Leaf Rag* (excerpt), 1899

In many pieces the composer emphasizes stability by keeping the pulse groups at each level consistent throughout an entire piece, or within a major section of a large work. In other pieces, changing the pulse groups from twos to threes or vice versa results in a heightening of rhythmic interest, an increase or decrease in tension, or—as in Example 3.6—a special emphasis on certain words of the text.

Example **3.6**   Claudio Monteverdi
            *L'Orfeo*, Act I
            "Leave the Mountains, Leave the Fountains," 1607

The first section, in a moderate tempo, has groups of twos at all levels, thus:

The second section shifts to a basic pulse group of threes at a very fast tempo, emphasizing a reference to dancing in the text. The third section (instruments only) carries on the tempo and basic meter of the second. In both these sections you can hear a second metric level that joins two of the basic three-pulse groups into longer two-pulse groups:

An interesting shift in metrical grouping occurs at the end of the instrumental line (heard twice). Two threes are regrouped into three twos:

becomes

This effect, called *hemiola*, can be found frequently in music as far apart in time and style as a medieval religious song and the tune "America" from *West Side Story*.

## METERS IN TWOS *AND* THREES

Except for the hemiola effect just described all the examples so far have had a basic pulse group of two *or* three consistently maintained, marking off equal time spans. In many pieces unequal time spans are created by mixing twos and threes, a procedure that tends to raise the level of tension for two reasons: (1) our musical conditioning leads us to expect that time will be marked off equally, and any expectation denied is a source of tension; and (2) such mixtures are harder to keep track of than consistent repetition of a single basic pulse group.

Example **3.7**   Indian music
                  *Rupak Tal* (excerpt)

At the beginning of the example the tabla (a pair of small drums) plays in groups of twos:

In the middle of the third group of twos the sarod (a plucked string instrument) interrupts this pattern and moves to a faster tempo with the meter grouped like this:

This pattern is clearly delineated by a descending melody with the highest and lowest pitches sounding on the first and last of the seven pulses. Note that the independence of the tabla established at the beginning of the example is maintained throughout, with the higher of the two drums operating almost as a free agent.

Sometimes equal and unequal time spans are woven together; small unequal spans can be repeated to produce larger spans of equal length, as in Example 3.8.

Example **3.8**　　Dave Brubeck
　　　　　　　　*Three to Get Ready* (excerpt), 1960

Following the piano introduction, which has four groups of three threes, there are two statements of the same musical material. Each statement has four clearly distinct sections; each section, in turn, has a pattern of 3 + 3 followed by 2 + 2 + 2 + 2. The first statement begins with the saxophone in threes, the second statement with the piano.

Example **3.9**　　Greek music
　　　　　　　　*San Kemena Palikari* (excerpt)

In this folk song each large metrical unit has a nine-pulse pattern of 2 + 2 + 2 + 3. The beginning of each of these units is emphasized by the bass; this sound will help you find and clap the pattern.

Example **3.10**　　Dave Brubeck
　　　　　　　　　*Blue Rondo Alla Turk* (excerpt), 1960

In this piece Brubeck uses a somewhat more complex pattern than in Example 3.8. It consists of nine pulses: 2 + 2 + 2 + 3 played three times, followed by 3 + 3 + 3. The complete pattern of thirty-six pulses is thus made up of four equal nine-pulse groups.

Example **3.11**　　Don Ellis
　　　　　　　　　*Turkish Bath* (excerpt), 1968

This work begins with sitar and tamboura (two Indian string instruments), in a pulseless free flow in time. At the end of this

*Ravi Shankar playing the sitar. At left,*
*a tabla; at right, a tamboura.*

opening section the sitar is joined by the band in a 2 + 2 + 3 pattern. The tempo is moderate, the pulse groups are well marked, and you should be able to clap the pattern easily.

Example **3.12**    Bulgarian music
              *Dilmano, Dilbero* (excerpt)

Unlike Examples 3.8–3.11, in which repetition created longer time spans of equal length, this piece involves a very fast, complex, and unequal mixture of two-pulse and three-pulse groups. While you may find it impossible to tap all the pulses, you are likely to sense the alternating short and long *units* of the twos and threes.

There are some other mixtures of twos and threes you could try clapping at different tempos. In a very fast tempo you will probably sense the short and long units, like those of Example 3.12. Try the following combinations:

Five-pulse: 2 + 3 or 3 + 2
Seven-pulse: 2 + 2 + 3 or 3 + 2 + 2 or 2 + 3 + 2

Create metrical "sentences" of two-pulse and three-pulse "words" in different orders. Perform the sentences by tapping them out.

Select phone numbers at random and form them into metrical groups with proper accents. Divide any digit higher than 3 into pulse groups of two or three. The phone number 325–7523, for example, would divide like this:

3   2    5          7          5    2   3

3 + 2 + (3 + 2) + (2 + 3 + 2) + (2 + 3) + 2 + 3
       or         or         or
   (2 + 3)  (2 + 2 + 3)  (3 + 2)
            or
       (3 + 2 + 2)

Are some phone numbers more interesting than others? Why?

If you have listened and clapped enough to follow the patterns presented so far you will enjoy trying to cope with the more complex patterns of Example 3.13.

Example **3.13**    Don Ellis
*New Horizons* (excerpt), 1968

After the brief beginning passage the piece falls into a fast 17-pulse pattern that becomes easier to pick up as the work progresses. The pattern is first grouped as (3 + 2) + (3 + 2) + (2 + 2) + 3, repeated four times, and then as (2 + 3) + (2 + 3) + (2 + 2) + 3, again repeated four times.

Invent short pieces for homemade percussion instruments, contrasting events flowing freely in time (as in Examples 2.2 and 2.5) with events that have a regular pulse.

## Metrical Conflict and Ambiguity

Examples 3.14–3.20 illustrate three types of metrical complication—*syncopation, superimposed meter*, and *suppressed meter*—that always create conflict or ambiguity, or both, and thus always increase the level of tension whenever they are used.

## SYNCOPATION

Syncopation and the tension-raising potential of its unexpectedly absent or conflicting accents was defined and illustrated earlier in this chapter (Example 3.2). Examples 3.14 and 3.15 offer further evidence of syncopation's unmistakable effect.

Example **3.14**   Peter Ilich Tchaikovsky
*Swan Lake*, "Valse" (excerpt), 1877

The normal accent of the fast three-pulse basic meter is contradicted by repeated stress on the second pulse of the group. The effect of conflict is heightened by an immediate return to the normal accent on the beginning of the first pulse:

Example **3.15**   William Bolcom
*Graceful Ghost* (excerpt), 1970

This ragtime-style piece has a highly intricate pattern of unexpected stresses at a meter level faster than the basic two-pulse group. If you tap the basic pulse you will hear many comparatively long sounds between the taps.

## SUPERIMPOSED METER

Superimposing a new meter grouping on a well-established meter level always creates metrical conflict—thus raising the level of tension—because it increases the number of musical events the listener must deal with simultaneously. The device is seldom used throughout a piece, since its effectiveness lies in the surprise of contrast the added meter provides to what has preceded it. Listen for this contrast in Examples 3.16–3.18.

*Steel band music is noted for its metrical intricacy and sophistication. These players were photographed in St. John, U.S. Virgin Islands.*

Example **3.16**    Gustav Mahler
*Symphony No. 2* ("Resurrection"), second movement (excerpt), 1894

This excerpt begins near the end of a section in which a basic pulse group of three and a faster level of two have been well established:

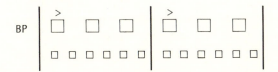

As the second section begins, a third level is added, in which each basic pulse is divided into threes as well:

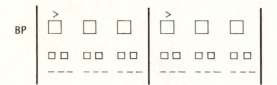

These three levels continue for some time before the original two-level simplicity is restored.

Example **3.17**    Brazilian music
Candomblé

At the beginning of this example no clear pulse emerges until the *agôgô* (an instrument constructed from two iron cones) establishes the following basic grouping of 2 + 2 + 3 + 2 + 3:

When the drums enter they add tension by performing irregular and inconsistent groupings of the twelve pulses. Then, midway through the piece, the drums settle into a regular three-pulse group while the agôgô continues with its original pattern:

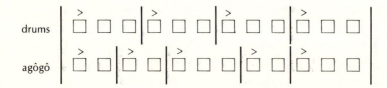

Example **3.18**     Cuban music
                     *Sutileza* (excerpt)

This is a fascinating example of superimposed meter. Over the basic rumba pattern of 3 + 3 + 2, the bongo-drum player superimposes complex patterns (mostly related to 2 + 2) in strong conflict with the basic meter. The effect is so powerful that you may find it difficult to pay attention to the voices and orchestra.

SUPPRESSED METER

Suppression of strong metrical emphasis often leads to ambiguity and the sort of uncertainty that is always a source of tension. The device has long been used in western music in styles as drastically different as a sixteenth-century Mass (Example 3.19) and a twentieth-century orchestral work (Example 3.20).

Example **3.19**     Josquin des Prez
                     *Missa Ave Maris Stella*, "Christe eleison," c. 1500

Here any sense of regular metrical grouping is minimized by the staggered entrances of the voices and their continuous rhythmic independence. Each musical idea is marked by syncopated figures that create shifting accents at irregular intervals.

Example **3.20**     Claude Debussy
                     *The Sea* (*La Mer*), second movement (excerpt), 1905

There are several metrical patterns in this excerpt, but none emerges as the dominant one, largely because there is little contrast of loudness and softness and, therefore, little or no accentuation of metrical groups. Debussy may have deliberately kept the meter flexible to capture the fluid rhythms of the sea.

## Synthesis

Sometimes a piece will include passages built on a single pulse group—twos or threes—as well as passages that combine twos and

threes either successively or in superimposition. Example 3.21
illustrates this kind of metrical complexity.

Example **3.21**    John McLaughlin
*Open Country Joy*, 1973

There are three clearly defined sections in this piece. The
third resembles the first, while the second is in strong contrast.
The opening section begins with most of the rhythmic activity
at two widely separated rates of speed, one quite slow (the
bass), the other quite fast (other instruments).

Q4    Are the main pulse groups of the bass twos or threes?
Q5    At the fast level of activity (mostly electric piano and snare
       drum), how many pulses are there to each main bass pulse? Are
       these pulses heard as a steady stream of twos or in unequal
       groups of twos and threes?

Soon after the beginning, a violin solo starts.

Q6    Is the rate of rhythmic activity (pace) of the solo faster, slower,
       or the same as the fast pulse rate of the beginning?
Q7    Do the pulse groups of the solo mostly coincide with or conflict
       with those surrounding it?
Q8    Are there any sections of the solo itself that lack metrical
       definition?

The second section begins after a rather long silence.

Q9    At the outset, and several times thereafter, a new pulse rate
       comes into play. Does it quicken or slow the pace?
Q10   Does the bass continue with its original slow pulse group, or
       shift to a faster 3 + 3 + 2?

The third section begins right after the end of the second,
with no intervening silence.

Q11   Does the overall rate of rhythmic activity shift gradually or
       abruptly at the beginning of this section?
Q12   Is the pulse rate of the violin solo generally the same as in the
       first section, or does it mostly coincide with the faster rate of
       other instruments?

Using a diagram like the ones we have employed in this chapter to represent pulse groups and levels of meter, try to outline the relationship between the slow bass pulse and the fast pulse of drums and piano in the first section.

Q13  How many levels of two-pulse metric groups can you find between these extremes?

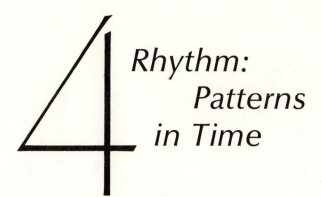

# Rhythm:
# Patterns
# in Time

Rhythm, as traditionally defined, takes in everything that has to do with the organization of musical elements in time. In this large sense rhythm is as much a part of music without pulse as it is of music with its pulses grouped into metric arrangements like those in Chapter 3. Rhythm includes pace, tempo, meter, and—beyond meter—an almost infinite number of ways in which long-short durations of sound and silence make up patterns in time. Here we will concentrate on a few simple examples of these rhythmic patterns in time, and for the purposes of this chapter, the terms *rhythm* and *rhythmic pattern* are used interchangeably.

Sometimes the rhythmic pattern and the basic pulse of a piece of music are almost identical, as in the opening phrases of "Twinkle, Twinkle Little Star":

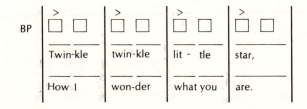

Except for the word "star" in the first phrase and "are" in the second, rhythm and the basic pulse coincide.

Try tapping the basic pulse of a familiar tune with your foot and clapping the rhythm of the words. Sometimes (as in "My country, 'tis of thee," for example) the pulse and the rhythmic pattern of the words will coincide almost as closely as in "Twinkle, Twinkle." But if you tap the basic pulse of "Swanee River," you will discover that there is a considerable difference between the pulse and the rhythmic pattern of the words. The foreground of the rhythm is heard and felt against the background of the metric pulse group, setting up a tension between rhythm and meter that is one of the most common sources of rhythmic interest:

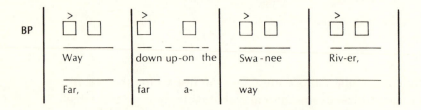

For all but one word, the normal spoken accents of the words coincide with the metrical accent or, in the case of "-on," the strong part (beginning) of an unaccented pulse. The exception, of course, is "riv-er." Its second syllable, never accented in speech, receives a double stress: its length, and the fact that it is syncopated—it falls on an unaccented part of the pulse. In calling attention so strongly to a weak syllable, the composer disrupts our expectations and sets up the kind of tension between meter and rhythm that we noted in several examples in Chapter 3. In "Swanee" the tension is relaxed at the end of the second line by having metrical accent and normal word accent coincide on "a-way."

## Recognizing Rhythmic Patterns

Rhythmic patterns are an important factor in musical organization because they are one of the chief means of providing both tension and repose. A sense of repose generally results when some one element supplies unity by remaining unchanged while other elements are undergoing significant modification. For instance, if the pitch of a musical idea is being changed while the rhythm remains clearly identifiable, the stability of the rhythm provides a norm for the listener that holds the tension down. On the other hand, when a rhythmic pattern is subjected to considerable variation (other elements aside), the unpredictability of the variation and the larger amount of information the listener must absorb can generate a great deal of tension. Naturally, if you as the listener cannot clearly identify a rhythmic pattern, you will have no way of knowing if the pattern remains unchanged or if it is varied, and you will thus miss the effect of these changing tension levels. All the examples in this chapter are designed to develop your ability to recognize rhythmic patterns.

UNIQUE PATTERNS

We will begin by concentrating on how rhythmic patterns function in brief passages, leaving until a later chapter the larger contexts in which these patterns figure prominently in providing unity and variety. In the following examples you will be asked to do two things: to match the rhythmic pattern you hear against one of the given diagrams, and to compare that pattern with the music that follows it. (Occasionally you will be asked other kinds of questions too.) Concentrate on the rhythmic pattern, not the pitches. You will find it helpful, once you have identified the correct pattern, to practice until you can tap it fluently.

Example **4.1**    Ludwig van Beethoven
*Piano Concerto No. 5* ("Emperor"), first movement (excerpt), 1809

Q1    Which line in the diagram on the next page matches the full orchestral entrance after the brief piano introduction?

Q2    After the basic pattern is played by the full orchestra the clarinet has a solo. Is the rhythm of the clarinet part
a. identical with the rhythm of the orchestral section?
b. very similar but not identical?
c. contrasting?

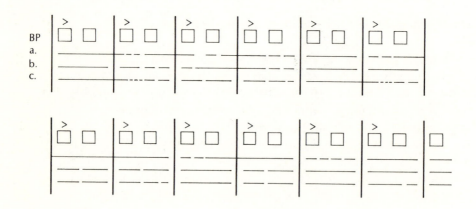

This picture is a unique collection of visual rhythms. What analogies can you draw between its rhythms and musical rhythms? (Pennsylvania Farmstead with Many Fences, c. 1830, anon.)

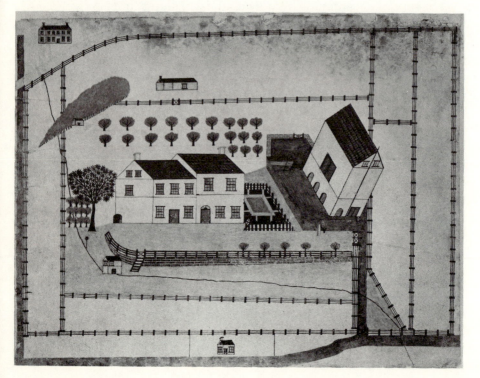

Example **4.2**    American music
            *John Henry* (excerpt)

Q3    Which line in the following diagram matches the beginning of
        the first verse after the guitar introduction?

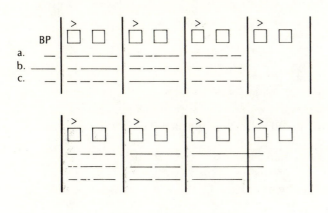

Q4    Is syncopation present in the excerpt?
Q5    Does the second verse begin with
        a. an identical rhythmic repetition?
        b. a similar, but varied pattern?
        c. a completely contrasting rhythm?

The basic pattern of the excerpt begins with an upbeat (or
*pickup*) on the word "John," which gives a sense of falling
forward to the first accented pulse ("*Hen*-ry"). The special lift a
pickup provides is a feature of many rhythmic patterns. If you
didn't notice the effect of the pickup, you may want to listen
again.

Example **4.3**    Johannes Brahms
            *Variations on a Theme by Haydn* (excerpt), 1873

This example contains six musical statements in this order:

        1. statement 1            4. statement 2 repeated
        2. statement 2            5. statement 3
        3. statement 1 repeated   6. statement 4

The following questions deal with the rhythmic pattern of the
first statement, and the relationship between it and the other
statements.

Q6 Which line in the following diagram matches the rhythm of the first statement?

Q7 Is the second statement
   a. rhythmically identical to the first?
   b. the same, but with a difference at the beginning?
   c. the same, but with a difference at the end?
   d. different from the first?

Q8 Does the rhythmic material of the third and fourth statements
   a. contrast with that of the first two?
   b. relate to the end of the first?
   c. relate to the beginning of the first?

Example **4.4**    Carole King and Gerry Goffin
                    *Snow Queen* (excerpt), 1972

The vocal line begins with two short sections that are almost like a statement and response. Most of the excerpt is in this statement-response format. The tempo of the basic pulse is slow.

Q9 Which line in the following diagram matches the first statement and response in the vocal line?

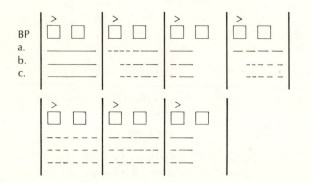

Q10   In the vocal line, is syncopation present in just the statement or in both statement and response?

Q11   Is the second vocal statement and response rhythmically identical to or different from the first?

Q12   In the vocal line, the pulse groups shift from twos to threes. Is the instrumental accompaniment consistently in twos or consistently in threes?

Example **4.5**   Wolfgang Amadeus Mozart
              *Piano Concerto No. 24*, K. 491
              first movement (opening), 1786

The following diagram represents a fragment of the rhythmic material that appears for the first time shortly after the beginning of the movement. During the course of the excerpt this fragment is used in a number of different ways.

Q13   Which line in the diagram matches the fragment?

Q14   Considering the fragment in all its forms, would you say that it is
      a. nearly always present?
      b. absent for a considerable time?
      c. present for only the first half of the excerpt?
      d. contrasted with a less memorable pattern that is used nearly as often?

Invent a rhythmic pattern based on metric groups totaling 12 pulses. Memorize it. Play variations on the pattern. Invent a contrasting pattern. Build a rhythm composition using the original pattern, its variations, and the contrasting pattern.

## DANCE RHYTHMS

So far we have been exploring particular rhythmic patterns created
by a composer for a specific composition; we have therefore been
studying one aspect of what makes a given piece unique. Let's
look now at dance rhythms—a class of distinctive rhythmic patterns
that exist independently of any particular piece and of any particular composer.

For obvious reasons the tempo, meter, and rhythmic patterns that
accompany the steps of a specific dance tend to become more or
less fixed. Any composer who wants to write a *habañera*, for example, would use one of the two rhythmic patterns that are characteristic of this traditional Cuban dance:

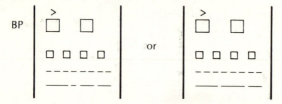

(Note that the second pattern groups the faster pulses in 3 + 3 + 2,
a rhythmic effect found frequently in jazz.)

> Example **4.6**  Emmanuel Chabrier
> *Habañera* (excerpt), 1885
>
> Example **4.7**  Claude Debussy
> *Preludes, Book 2*, "La Puerta del Vino" (excerpt), 1910
>
> In comparing Examples 4.6 and 4.7, notice that Chabrier keeps
> the dance patterns to the fore, while Debussy keeps them
> subdued, suggesting rather than declaring their presence.

Many times, in concert music, a composer will keep the essence of
a dance's rhythms, but will treat the basic pattern with considerable
freedom. In such cases, the listener's familiarity with the basic
pattern sets up expectations that the composer may or may not
choose to fulfill; the composer thus creates the possibility of
thwarted expectations—always a rich source of interest and tension.
Listen to Examples 4.8–4.11 from this point of view.

*A sampler of dances and dancers. (Left: Village Dancers, c. 1650, by L. P. Boithard; below: Children Dancing, 1948, by Robert Gwathmey; above: Fox Trot, 1961, by Andy Warhol)*

Example **4.8**    George Frideric Handel
*Keyboard Suite No. 11*, Sarabande (theme), 1733

Example **4.9**    George Frideric Handel
*Keyboard Suite No. 13*, Sarabande, 1733

The *sarabande* is a rather dignified dance with a rhythmic pattern based on three slow pulses. In the first of these two sarabandes, Handel treats the pattern simply and straightforwardly; in the second, his treatment is far freer and more elaborate.

## OSTINATO

Not a pattern in the same sense as a dance rhythm, which *stays* recognizable from piece to piece, the ostinato is a rhythmic pattern—often fused with a melody—that *becomes* recognizable by being repeated more or less continuously throughout a given composition. Thus, though the pattern of any ostinato is often unique to the piece in which it occurs, its principle remains always the same. Ostinatos serve as an organizing device in the music of most cultures, functioning as a kind of accompaniment. Up to a certain point, repetition of an ostinato produces security and repose; beyond that point repetition tends to raise the level of tension by its very insistence. As an accompaniment, an ostinato affords another source of tension, as illustrated in Example 4.10.

Example **4.10**    Terry Riley
*A Rainbow in Curved Air* (excerpt), 1971

Here the ostinato competes for attention with the material being accompanied, and the listener must concentrate on both.

Some of the following examples employ the characteristic rhythmic patterns, often repeated, of certain dances. Others are based on the repetition of an ostinato. The following exercise is designed to help you distinguish between the two.

*Pont des Arts, a bridge in Paris. Its repeating understructure functions somewhat as an ostinato does in music.*

Q15  Listen to Examples 4.11–4.17. Beside each, write a *D* if it is a dance pattern, an *O* if it is an ostinato.*

Example **4.11**  Music of Senufo

Example **4.12**  Frédéric Chopin

Example **4.13**  Bill Chase

Example **4.14**  Pierre Attaingnant

Example **4.15**  Carl Orff

Example **4.16**  Indian music

Example **4.17**  Johann Sebastian Bach

* Some of the titles in these examples would give away the answer before you heard the piece, so in this case the titles are included with the answers at the end of the book.

Invent an ostinato pattern. In class or small groups try performing two or more ostinatos together, adding and dropping one at a time. Shape the piece by making things louder or softer. Make changes as needed to develop a piece that works well.

Compose a short percussion piece for three players, using as one element either a dance pattern or an ostinato. Try to build up some tension. Invent your own notation as needed.

Do some investigation of the relationship between music and dances. Try to find and listen to pieces with such dance titles as pavane, minuet, cakewalk, waltz, rumba, etc., and see how they compare with dictionary descriptions. Pick out a dance that interests you particularly and study it in some detail.

By now, it should be fairly obvious to you that creating and perceiving music can be a complicated affair. If you have been learning to listen closely and well, you will have gained some skill in coping with the complications discussed in this chapter: the intricacies of rhythm versus meter, of continuity versus contrast of rhythmic patterns, and the frequent tension in the conflict of these things as a composition unfolds. These listening skills will stand you in good stead as you increase and sharpen them in the chapters to come.

## Synthesis

Example 4.18 combines several of the topics of this chapter—unique rhythmic patterns, dance patterns, and ostinato—together with one aspect of music flowing freely in time (Chapter 2).

Example **4.18**    Henry Purcell
*Dido and Aeneas*, "Thy Hand, Belinda" and "Dido's Lament," 1689

RECITATIVE:

Thy hand, Belinda, darkness shades me,
On thy bosom let me rest.
More I would, but death invades me;
Death is now a welcome guest.

AIR:

When I am laid in earth,
May my wrongs create
No trouble in thy breast;
Remember me, but ah! forget my fate.

In the recitative, rhythm is a free-flowing response to the words, without the regularity of metric pulse groups, but the entire air is metrically organized, often with rhythmic patterns repeated.

Q16   Which words accompany this pattern:

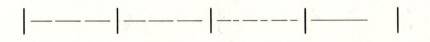

Q17   A bit later, the following pattern emerges (with silences in the vocal line indicated by the blank spots in the diagram). What are the accompanying words?

Q18   As the air begins, the orchestra commences an ostinato in the bass which has the following pitch contour and rhythm. How many times does this ostinato occur?

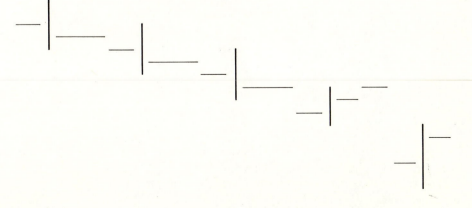

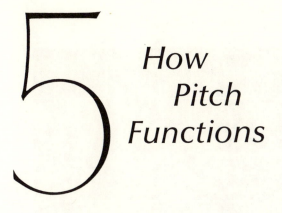

# How
# Pitch
# Functions

Music's domain is, of course, the sound space within which the human ear can hear, a spectrum usually described in terms of frequencies. A *frequency* is the rate of to-and-fro vibration per second by a sounding body (such as a violin string, a drumhead, or the vocal cords). The slowest frequency the ear can hear is around 20 vibrations or cycles per second, and the fastest is around 18,000.* Below the audio range we hear separate pulses; above it are ultrasonic frequencies beyond the reach of the human ear. In Example 5.1, an oscillator of a synthesizer sweeps this entire spectrum.

Example **5.1** Synthesizer demonstration
of the audible frequency spectrum

Throughout this example sound is being generated. The break halfway through is the point at which the oscillator sweeps into the ultrasonic range and then returns.

---

* Frequencies are now usually expressed in units called *hertz* (abbreviated *Hz*). One hertz is equal to one cycle per second; 20 Hz is thus the same frequency as 20 cycles per second, and 18 kHz is the same as 18,000 cycles per second.

*Played on a trumpet, the A above middle C produces a sound wave that "looks" like this.*

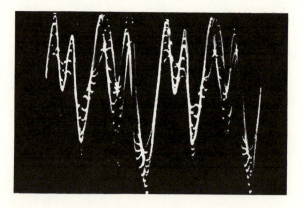

As you listen to the frequencies generated by the synthesizer, your ears are responding to them as *pitches*. For reasons not entirely clear, though they go deep into our conditioning, we say that the slower the frequency, the "lower" the pitch; and the faster the frequency, the "higher" the pitch. We use this convention despite the fact that it has no physical validity. All sound waves—no matter what their source, and no matter how fast or slow—occupy the same physical space; high pitches are not above our heads nor are low ones at our feet.

## Range and Register

The portion of the pitch spectrum within which all the pitches of a composition fall is called the *range* of that composition. The way pitch is used within the range has a good deal to do with tension and repose levels. Theoretically, composers have always had available to them all the pitches they can discriminate within the total spectrum. But not until the advent of electronic sound production and its influence on the use of conventional instruments have composers exploited this full range.

Example **5.2**   Ilhan Mimaroglu
*Agony* (excerpt), 1965

In this piece Mimaroglu, like many composers of the last decade or more, exploits the available pitch space in a way that reflects the expansiveness of modern technology. Moving freely about the entire spectrum in this fashion puts pitch in a far broader perspective than that of older times and other cultures.

In more traditional kinds of music, range is exploited in more limited and focused ways, whether the range is wide or narrow. For reasons we can only guess at, extremes of range—very wide or very narrow—generally create more tension than ranges of moderate scope. In a piece with a very narrow range fewer pitches are available; each pitch must therefore be repeated more often, and after a certain amount of repetition, tension rises. In a piece of very wide range the tension may arise from the listener's "stretching" empathetically with the performer for the very high or very low pitches.

Between the lowest and the highest pitches of the range lies the average pitch area, called the *register*. Sometimes it is low compared with the total range; sometimes it is high. Again, register seems to be related to tension, with a very high or very low register generating more tension than one in the middle of the range.

The rate at which a range is covered also affects our sense of musical tension. A wide range swept in a short time span makes the listener strongly aware of pitch extremes; more tension is therefore likely to result than if the same range were unfolded over a longer time span. The opposite is true of a narrow range: covering it quickly has little effect, while a slow presentation raises more tension. Examples 5.3–5.8 will help you in listening for the effects of range and register, and rates of change within them.

Example **5.3** Krzysztof Penderecki
*Capriccio for Violin and Orchestra* (excerpt), 1967

You will easily hear that the solo violin part covers a very wide range, one that extends to the lowest and highest pitches the performer can produce.

Q1 Is the extent of this range first set out by wide leaps or by a more gradual sweep?

Q2   Does most of the solo cluster around one portion (register) of the range, or does it generally cover a wide span?

Example **5.4**   Music of Senufo
*Men's Song*

The range of this piece is very narrow, almost like expressive speech.

Q3   Compared with the usual range of men's voices, is the register high, low, or mid-range?

Q4   Does the song move to its highest pitch more than once?

Example **5.5**   Krzysztof Penderecki
*The Devils of Loudon*, Act I, Scene 8 (excerpt), 1969

The contrast between this example and the preceding one is startling. The range of the soprano part almost demands the impossible of the singer.

Q5   Does the singer reach her highest pitch by a leap from mid-range or from an already high level?

Q6   The passages that begin and end the soprano part contrast in register. How?

Example **5.6**   Johannes Brahms
*Symphony No. 1*, fourth movement (excerpt), 1876

The range of the principal tune is quite narrow—just a few pitches wider than the Senufo song of Example 5.4, though it uses more pitches within that range.

Q7   Is the register mostly mid-range, high, or low?

Q8   Is the range swept gradually or rapidly?

Example **5.7**   Edgard Varèse
*Density 21.5* (excerpt), 1936

Varèse asks the performer to cover nearly the complete range of the flute in the course of this excerpt.

Q9   Are the extremes of the range reached by gradual sweeps or by large leaps?

Example **5.8**   Duke Ellington
*Caravan* (excerpt), 1937

70

The principal tune is in the right hand of the piano part.

Q10   Is the range of this part unfolded quickly or gradually?
Q11   In which of the four sections of the tune is the highest pitch
      reached?

## Pitch Systems

Examples 5.2–5.8 share the elements of range and register. Beyond
that, however, the way in which their pitches are used divides them
sharply into two groups. Examples 5.4, 5.6, and 5.8 operate within
the timeless, nearly universal *pitch-system convention*, in which any
particular pitch system consists of a selected number of pitches
that have a certain fixed relationship to each other. Examples 5.2,
5.3, and to a lesser extent 5.7, operate outside the pitch-system
convention. By choosing to dispense with this convention, many
composers today have extended musical possibilities in ways that
challenge ears steeped in the particular pitch system of their own
culture.

Our own ears are conditioned, of course, by the major-minor
pitch system (page 73) that has been central to western music for
several centuries. This system is only one of many that have
developed in different regions at different periods in different
cultures. Although various pitch systems (or *modes*) differ widely
in number of pitches and in relationships between the pitches,
none of them is inherently better than another, and all are potent
sources of tension and repose in the shaping of music.

All modes have three things in common:

1. A selection of pitches within the pitch space of an octave
   (Example 5.9).
2. Established distances (or *intervals*) between the pitches in
   this octave span.
3. The tendency, within any piece, for one of its pitches to
   become the focus and final arrival point of all the other
   pitches—to become a *tonic*.

Example **5.9**   Synthesizer demonstration of octaves

All the sounds you hear in Example 5.9 are octaves, intervals that
are characterized by their quality of "sound-alikeness," even
though their actual pitches differ. This quality of *octave identity*
is the basis for dividing up pitch space within any pitch system:
every pitch is fixed in distance from every other pitch within the
space of an octave; this pattern of fixed intervals then repeats from
octave to octave through the available range.

Even if you don't play the piano, you can confirm the fact of octave
identity for yourself at a keyboard. Look for the repeating pattern of
black keys—two together, then three together. Go up and down
the keyboard striking the left-hand key in each group of two black
keys; you will be playing octaves and it will be evident to you that
they are sound-alikes. To confirm the fact that pitches fixed at the
same distance from each other within each octave form a repeating
pattern, play the whole group of two-plus-three black keys from
left to right at all the places it occurs. You will hear the sameness
of each five-pitch group, as well as the octave identity of the
corresponding pitches in each group.

THE PENTATONIC MODE

When you played the group of two-plus-three black keys, you were
playing the basic five-pitch order of one of the oldest known pitch
systems—the *pentatonic mode*.

Example **5.10**   Indian music
                   *Salutation Song* (excerpt)

This song uses primarily the first three pitches of the pentatonic
mode, reaching the fourth and fifth pitches only briefly. You
will easily recognize the primary importance of the lowest
pitch as the point to which the other pitches constantly return.
A pitch with this focal role is the *tonic*.

Q12   How many times does the singer reach beyond the third pitch?

Example **5.11**    Chinese music
*Wild Geese Alighting on the Sandy Shore* (excerpt)

This song also uses the pentatonic system, but it is more complex than Example 5.10 in two ways: more than one pitch
seems to function as a tonic, and there are several occurrences
of a pitch that does not fit into the pentatonic mode. This added
pitch, which can be regarded as an auxiliary tone, creates
tension because it is unexpected; it thus adds drama and
intensity to the passage. Most pitch systems use auxiliary tones
as tension-raisers.

Q13   Are the two instruments playing different pitch successions
(melodies), or are they simply playing two versions of the same
melody, one more elaborate than the other?

## THE MAJOR AND MINOR MODES

For over two centuries western music has used a pitch system
based on dividing the pitch space within an octave into twelve
equidistant pitches. The interval between each of these pitches is
called a *half-step*. At the keyboard, begin with the pitch C (see
Figure 1) and move up or down to the nearest key, white or black.
Continue in this way until you reach the C an octave above or
below, and you will have played the twelve pitches most commonly
used in western music. You can establish the sound and feel of
identity from octave to octave by continuing to play this key-to-
next-key pattern between all the C's on the keyboard.

Figure 1

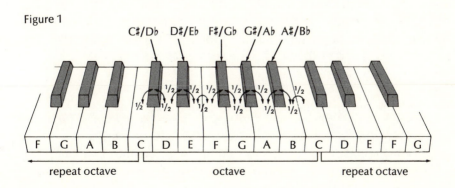

In playing this twelve-pitch *scale* (any ladder-like, pitch-to-next-pitch arrangement of a set of selected pitches) you may think that the pitch relationships you hear don't have much in common with most of the tunes you know. The reason is that only seven of these twelve pitches, in a variety of modes, have been used traditionally as the actual basic pitch material of a given composition, with the other five pitches serving in different auxiliary ways. Two of the possible seven-pitch modes have been of primary importance in western music for the last three hundred years. They are called the *major mode* and the *minor mode*, and they are both very familiar to your ears, whether or not you have ever heard their names. To hear the major mode arranged as a scale, start with a C at the keyboard and play in succession all the white keys up or down through the next C. To hear the basic minor mode in scale form, do the same thing with the white keys A through A except for the key G; instead of G, play the black key just above it (G-sharp). In the major scale you played, C is the central pitch—the tonic; similarly, in the minor scale the tonic is A. To test just how strongly our ear needs to arrive at the tonic, try playing these two scales again, stopping on B for the C major scale and on G-sharp for the A minor scale. Do you find it possible to resist finally going on to the C and the A?

The major and minor modes sound quite different from each other because their interval structure— the distance from pitch to pitch—differs. Figure 2 shows that structure in half-steps (key-to-next-key, black or white) and whole-steps (two half-steps, of course). It should be evident that you could start these patterns on any one of the twelve pitches within the octave. If you did this you would be *transposing* to the scales of each of the twelve major and twelve minor "keys" used in much of our music. Each starting pitch becomes a new tonic, and wherever you start, the sound of "majorness" or "minorness" remains because the *relationship* between the pitches—their interval structure—is the same.

Although major and minor modes are closely intertwined in a great many compositions, they can be made to function in a kind of contrast that creates a good deal of tension between the two.

Figure 2

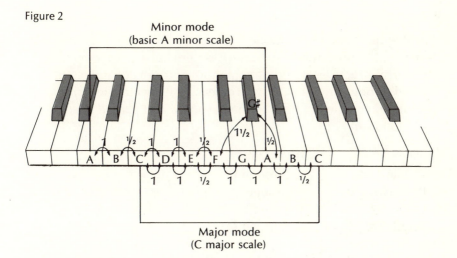

Minor mode
(basic A minor scale)

Major mode
(C major scale)

Example 5.12 illustrates this tension, as well as the difference in sound between the two modes.

Example **5.12**　Franz Schubert
*The Winter Journey*, "Good Night" (excerpt), 1827

This verse of the song begins in minor, moves to major, and returns to minor. Here is the German text:*

Was soll ich länger weilen, dass man mich trieb' hinaus?
Lass irre Hunde heulen vor ihres Herren Haus!
Die Liebe liebt das Wandern, Gott hat sie so gemacht,
von Einem zu dem Andern, Gott hat sie so gemacht.
Die Liebe liebt das Wandern, fein Liebchen, gute Nacht!
von Einem zu dem Andern, fein Liebchen, gute Nacht!

Q14　Does the change from minor to major occur at line 2 or line 3?
Q15　Does the change back to minor happen at the next-to-last line or the last line?

* Translation: Why should I tarry longer, if I am to be rejected? Let mad dogs howl in front of their master's house! Love loves wandering, God has made it so. From one to the other, God has made it so. Love loves wandering, dear sweetheart, good night! From one to the other, dear sweetheart, good night!

## MORE MODES

While the major and minor modes have played the most prominent role in the past three hundred years of western music, other modes with interval structures different from those of the major and minor prevailed during earlier centuries. To hear how the most important ones sound, you can go back to the keyboard and play *all white keys* as follows:

| Mode | White Keys |
|------|------------|
| Dorian | D through D |
| Phrygian | E through E |
| Lydian | F through F |
| Mixolydian | G through G |

As with the major and minor modes, you can start a scale in any of these modes on any of the twelve available pitches, using black and white keys as necessary to preserve the relationships of half- and whole-steps. You should have no trouble in figuring out the pattern of half-steps and whole-steps of each mode.

After three centuries of little or no use, two of these modes, the Dorian and Mixolydian, have recently been incorporated with major and minor in a great deal of popular music, probably because of the influence of the blues.

Example **5.13**   Lightnin' Hopkins
*Bad Luck and Trouble* (excerpt)

The so-called blue notes (auxiliary tones) you can hear in this example modify the major mode so that it sounds somewhat Mixolydian or Dorian.

> Choose a song you know well and try to play its melody on the piano, the guitar, or any other instrument.
>
> Select six pitches at random within an octave and a half on any instrument. Arrange them in different ways (including repeating a pitch) to create interesting melodies. Which arrangements of pitches seem the most successful? Can you tell why?

Compose three melodies using the black keys of the piano. For each melody, establish a different pitch as the tonic center. How did you accomplish this?

Write another black-key melody that avoids any sense of a tonic center, organizing it mainly by a rhythmic pattern. How did you avoid creating a tonic?

# *Chords*

Up to now our discussion of pitch systems has been in terms of *successions* of pitches—and in many musical cultures a one-after-the-other succession is almost the only way pitches are ever used. Western music, however, has developed the *simultaneous combination* of pitches very extensively, ranging from the simplicity of just two pitches sounded together to the extreme density and complexity of the combinations you have heard in some of the examples (Examples 1.1–1.7, for instance). In an introductory study, we can only discuss a few of the simplest simultaneous combinations (or chords) commonly used in the major and minor modes.

### TRIADS AND SEVENTH CHORDS

A *chord*, theoretically speaking, is any set of three or more different pitches sounded simultaneously. In the major and minor modes, however, chords are built up by intervals of thirds (Figure 3).

Figure 3

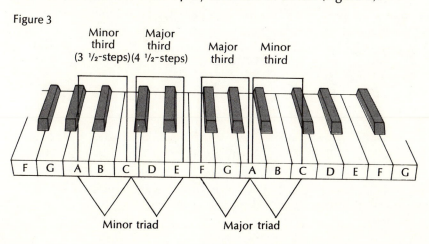

Minor third (3 ½-steps)  Major third (4 ½-steps)  Major third  Minor third

Minor triad          Major triad

At the keyboard, if you play the pitches C-E-G, F-A-C, or G-B-D simultaneously, you are playing *major triads*—chords with a major third on the bottom and a minor third on top. If you play the pitches D-F-A, E-G-B, or A-C-E, you are playing *minor triads*—with a minor third on the bottom and a major third on top. (Actually, any pitch of each of these chords can be the top or the bottom pitch without destroying the chord's identity. For example, try playing C-E-G, then E-G-C, then G-C-E.) Each of these triads may be extended by adding another third on top, making a *seventh chord:* C-E-G-B (or B-flat), G-B-D-F (or F-sharp), D-F-A-C, etc.* Triads and seventh chords form the basic material of what is conventionally called *harmony*. We tend to think of these chords as agreeable sounds, in and of themselves, and you may want to experiment by building them on different pitches—seeing how they sound with now one pitch, now another above or below—or by duplicating a chord in more than one octave at a time.

FUNCTIONAL RELATIONSHIPS

The main point about chords, however, is not their structure, nor their separate identity, nor how well they may sound individually, but how they function in relationship to each other—that is, what their role is as an organizing power in a composition, and as a means of raising or lowering the level of tension. To discuss function in even the most basic way we need a little more terminology: the names and numbers conventionally used to identify the chords in a mode. To keep things simple, we will stay in the major mode and the C major scale:

| C | D | E | F | G | A | B |
|---|---|---|---|---|---|---|
| tonic | supertonic | mediant | subdominant | dominant | submediant | leading tone |
| I | II | III | IV | V | VI | VII |

* The term "seventh," like "second," "third," "fourth," "fifth," and "sixth," describes the interval formed by the bottom and top pitches.

78

The most important chord is the tonic (I). Once established, it is the focal point, the goal of motion, the center of repose. Any move away from the tonic raises tension—an expectation of return to it. In fact, the whole edifice of functional relationships between chords is an intricate network of expectations: what chord will follow what chord on the way home to the tonic. For any listener who is tuned in to these expectations there is a never-ending flow of tension-repose effects as expectations are raised, fulfilled, delayed, or denied.

The next most important chord is the dominant (V). Its function is to introduce the tonic, and these two chords alone can establish the tonal base or center—the key.

Example **5.14**　W. A. Morris and Z. Morris
*Jimmy Brown the Newsboy* (excerpt)

The first verse, after the instrumental introduction, begins with the tonic, changes to the dominant on the word "Brown" and back to the tonic on "town."

*If this painting were a composition in the major or
minor mode, which figure would be the tonic?*
(The Last Supper, c. 1498, by Leonardo da Vinci)

Q16    On what words do the changes take place in the second verse? the third?

Q17    Does the pattern continue in the same way or does it change?

A third chord, the subdominant (IV), is joined with tonic and dominant in many well-known tunes. Sometimes it moves directly to the tonic, sometimes it introduces the dominant on the way to the tonic, and sometimes it interrupts the direct motion of dominant to tonic.

Example **5.15**    Johnny Winter
Rock and Roll (excerpt), 1973

This piece begins with an instrumental introduction on the tonic chord only, firmly establishing it as the center. The rest of the excerpt consists of two verses of the song. Each verse has the chord structure outlined in the following diagram, which shows how long each chord lasts in terms of the two-pulse basic meter. The tempo is slow.

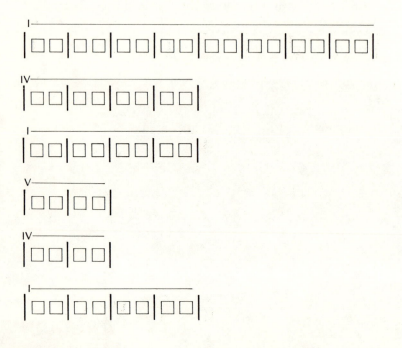

In the fifth line of the diagram the subdominant (IV) chord interrupts the expected direct succession of V to I, thus introducing a brief moment of tension. During the second verse there is less tension at this point because the surprise has already been heard.

Q18 On what words of the text in verses 1 and 2 does this chord change take place?

Q19 Following are lines from three familiar songs. How many chord changes are there in each line? On what words do they come?
a. Mary had a little lamb, little lamb, little lamb
b. Silent night, holy night, all is calm, all is bright
c. Old MacDonald had a farm, ee-i-ee-i-o

Example **5.16**    Frédéric Chopin
*Prelude*, Op. 28, No. 7, 1839

In Example 5.15 we noted the brief interruption of the expected V-I chord progression. In this piece there is a somewhat more dramatic harmonic happening. As shown in the diagram, a regular alternation of dominant-to-tonic is interrupted by an unexpected appearance of the VI chord. The tension thus raised is gently lowered by a commonly used succession of VI-II-V-I.

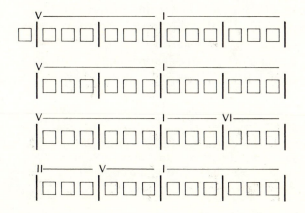

Example **5.17**  A. P. Carter
            *Salty Dog* (excerpt)

The chord succession at the end of Example 5.15 is one used in a great many older pieces. In *Salty Dog*, we hear it in especially compressed and repetitive fashion. The diagram again shows the chords heard on the pulses of the two-pulse basic meter, in a rather fast tempo. (The signs **‖:** and **:‖** at beginning and end indicate that everything between is repeated, in this case each successive verse.)

In this sequence each chord from VI on has the feel of introducing the next, and there is, in fact, a kind of dominant-to-tonic relationship between VI and II and II and V, as well as between the real V and I.

Q20   Does the chord succession change or stay the same during the instrumental sections?

Your ear has probably told you by now that these simple chord relationships are like many you hear in a wide range of music. Once having grasped the idea of the *function* of chords, you will have a basis for distinguishing between the expected and the unexpected, and for sensing the power of chord succession in both raising and resolving tension.

Devise a sequence of chords that pleases you. After you learn it well, add a melody to the chords. Play the piece on your instrument, or ask a friend to play the chords or melody with you.

*We wouldn't know what time it was if any part of
this clockwork failed to function properly in
relation to every other part.*

## Density

### INTERVAL CONTENT

For most of us, chords and their functional relationships are the
most familiar aspect of simultaneous sound. But much of western
music, both in the centuries before about 1700 and in most of the
new developments since 1900, has dealt with intervals rather than
chords. The ways in which intervals are used range from closely
controlled systems of tension-repose relationships to the use of all

intervals freely and unsystematically. Examples 5.18–5.22 touch on the extremes of contrast between these two limits. They also suggest the role of *density*—the number of pitches sounding simultaneously—in creating contrast and establishing levels of tension or repose.

Example **5.18**   Anonymous, *Ductia*

In this fourteenth-century dance there are only two pitches sounding at a time, resulting in a consistently low density. Among the simultaneous intervals sounded, only the octave and fifth serve as points of repose; all other intervals move toward them, setting up varying degrees of tension on the way.

Example **5.19**   Heinrich Isaac
  *Carmen saecularis* (excerpt), c. 1500

This piece uses a slightly larger variety of intervals than *Ductia*, and includes the third, as well as the fifth and octave, as a principal point of repose. It also has contrasts in density, from a low of two pitches at a time to a high of four.

Example **5.20**   Carlo Gesualdo
  *I Die in Despair (Moro Lasso)* (excerpt), c. 1600

This song has considerably greater interval variety and density than either of the preceding examples. Intervals of the second and seventh are used to create the high levels of musical tension that match the despairing text: "Alas, she who could give me life gives me death." The density ranges from a low of one pitch to a high of five.

Example **5.21**   Igor Stravinsky
  *The Rite of Spring*, "The Sacrifice" (excerpt), 1913

In this piece, tension does not rise or fall because of any particular set of intervals. Rather, the tension is a matter of changes in density—from a low of ten to twelve to a high of forty or more pitches at a time. The prevailing impression is of high-density, high-tension sound, rather vaguely based on a pitch center.

Example **5.22**   Pierre Boulez
            *The Hammer Without a Master*
            (*Le marteau sans maître*) (excerpt), 1957

As in Example 5.21, there is no hierarchy of intervals, and even less sense of any pitch as a tonic center. Changes in density are a frequent and important source of interest.

## MICROTONES

Throughout our discussion of pitch systems, the smallest interval used has been the half-step. Other musics—for instance that of China (as in Example 5.11)—have habitually used smaller intervals, sometimes called "microtones," but in western music they were used only occasionally before the twentieth century.

Example **5.23**   Paul Beaver and Bernard Krause
            *Quarter Tones*, 1968

Example **5.24**   Paul Beaver and Bernard Krause
            *White Sound Composition*, 1968

The first of these examples (both from *The Nonesuch Guide to Electronic Music*) presents an illustration of quarter tones, intervals half the size of a half-step. The second demonstrates "white sound" (or "white noise"), which is the sound of all frequencies at once. Here we no longer hear distinct pitches; the sense of high or low results from selective filtering, in which only limited bands of the total pitch spectrum are allowed to come through.

Example **5.25**   *Composition*
            from *The Nonesuch Guide to Electronic Music*, 1968

We close the circle of our exploration of pitch by returning to the point with which we began in Mimaroglu's *Agony*—we hear a composition that roams freely over the full spectrum of frequencies, using all the interval possibilities including microtones and segments of full-frequency white sound.

## Synthesis

No single piece could summarize the variety of pitch functions discussed in this chapter. The song in Example 5.26 involves some considerations of range and register, major and minor, and tonic and dominant.

Example **5.26**     Franz Schubert
                     *Death and the Maiden*, c. 1815

Here is the German text:*

DAS MÄDCHEN:

Vorüber, ach vorüber, geh' wilder Knochenmann!
Ich bin noch jung; geh, Lieber,
    und rühre mich nicht an,
    und rühre mich nicht an.

DER TOD:

Gieb deine Hand, du schön und zart Gebild,
bin Freund, und komme nich zu strafen.
Sei gutes Muths! ich bin nicht wild,
sollst sanft in meinen Armen schlafen.

Q21   Which part of the song, Death's or the Maiden's, has the lower register? the wider range?

Q22   On which words of the text does the Maiden's voice reach the highest point of its range?

Q23   The piano introduction and conclusion use tonic and dominant chords in the same order, same rhythmic pattern, and same register, but one section is minor and the other is major. Which is which?

* Translation: *The Maiden:* Pass by, pass by, fierce Death! I am still young; go, fellow, and touch me not, touch me not. *Death:* Give me your hand, fair and gentle creature; I am a friend, and come not to punish. Be of good spirit! I am not fierce. You shall sleep softly in my arms.

Q24 Two chords, tonic and dominant, are used in the piano introduction, the rhythmic pattern of which is given below. Add the
symbol I or V wherever you hear the tonic or dominant chord.

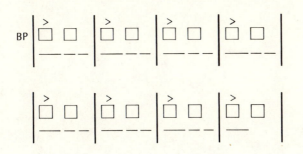

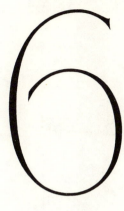

# Foreground and Background

Most of the music we listen to is complex, with more than one thing usually vying for our attention at any one time. This is so generally true that listening to a work like Example 6.1 is a startling revelation of just how much interest there can be in a single-line (*monophonic*) piece.

Example **6.1**  Japanese music
*Bell Ringing in the Empty Sky* (excerpt)

With no competition from other instruments, this player of the shakuhachi, an end-blown vertical flute of bamboo, explores its full possibilities—every shade of loudness, pitch, range, and tone color.

Q1  Which of these factors contribute(s) most to the illusion that the music advances and recedes?

*A shakuhachi, the Japanese flute you hear in Example 6.1.*

Improvise some single-line melodies on the piano or any other instrument. Exploit changes in loudness, range, and, if possible, tone color. If you use a piano, try different pressures on the keys. You might depress the damper pedal (the one on the right), then pluck the strings with a pick, fingernail, paper clip, or some other handy device.

Single-line music is an infrequent part of our experience. More commonly, we face the problem of which of several things to listen to. In a song, for instance, shall we concentrate on the singer's line and words, the pianist playing chords, the bass with a line of its own, or the rhythmic support of the drums? If we ignore everything but the vocal line, we may be missing interesting things in the other parts. Learning to concentrate on each of the parts, then on their relationship to each other, and, finally, taking in everything at once may mean many listenings, but the reward of enriched experience makes the effort well worthwhile. One way to begin is to pay simultaneous attention to an obvious musical foreground and a less obvious background.

*In terms of dominance, there is no competition for our attention here. The painting is foreground alone, and we are conscious of nothing but the head. (Senecio, 1922, by Paul Klee)*

## Musical Foreground

SINGLE DOMINANCE

To say that a musical element is in the foreground is to say that it dominates its surroundings by being heard more prominently than anything else. It can dominate in many ways: by being loudest, by being the most active line in rhythm or pitch, by being lowest or highest, or by being distinctly different in sound. Simply put, any musical idea will dominate if it is the most evident or most interesting thing going on at the moment. Examples 6.2–6.5 explore some of the characteristics of musical dominance.

> Example **6.2** Johann Sebastian Bach
> *Cantata No. 140*, "Sleepers Awake"
> Chorale, "Zion Hears the Watchman Calling"
> (excerpt), c. 1731

There are three independent lines in this excerpt—the high strings, the low strings, and the unison tenors. During the first section only the high and low strings are heard, with the former clearly dominant; they are louder, more active, and altogether more interesting. The lower line has its own interest, as you will note if you focus on it, but the top line commands more attention. When the tenors enter in the second section, try paying attention to each line in turn.

Q2 Which of the three lines dominates in the second section?
Q3 What is it that raises the level of tension at this point?

> Example **6.3** Mike Kamen and Marty Fulterman
> *Beside You* (excerpt), 1970

This excerpt is for vocalist, guitar, oboes, and cello. Although the guitar is more active in both rhythm and melody, you will probably find that the human voice, carrying the main melody and the words, is almost irresistibly dominant, as it is in most songs. (Listen to the guitar part. Why can its pace be considered both faster and slower than the pace of the voice?)

> Example **6.4** Darius Milhaud
> *The Creation of the Earth* (excerpt), 1923

*Although there is plenty of detail in the background, the foreground figure of General Washington is clearly dominant. (c. 1794, by Frederick Kemmelmeyer)*

This work is written for a chamber (small) orchestra that includes percussion and saxophone. The excerpt opens with strings and piano playing undulating figures at a fast meter level, while the saxophone plays a smooth, sustained melody with timpani punctuating lightly. This group is joined by trumpets and, later, trombones, culminating in a climax. The saxophone dominates for three reasons: it has the principal melody, it is louder than the other instruments, and its tone color is very distinctive. Although the piano and strings are more active, their sameness of material and motion tends to make them recede in interest.

Example **6.5** Franz Schubert
     *The Little Village (Dörfchen)* (excerpt), 1817

There are four voice parts in this piece, all moving together in rhythmic unison.

Q4 Which voice part emerges as the dominating one? Why?

## SHIFTING DOMINANCE

Example **6.6**    Peter Ilich Tchaikovsky
*1812 Overture* (excerpt), 1880

This excerpt begins with a great deal of activity, as various ideas compete for attention in constantly shifting foreground-background relationships, eventually reaching a peak of conflict. Suddenly there is but a single melody, powerfully reinforced in various octaves by strings and winds. After this passage finally winds down, the outburst of competing sounds and ideas reaches an even greater climax than before. The single-line passage, which functions as a link between what precedes and follows it, attains its dramatic effect largely by contrast with what has come before: after the tumult of competing ideas, the stark singularity of only one thing to listen to—foreground alone.

Theoretically, the number of instruments and voices that can be combined in any composition is unlimited, but when the ear is presented with more than it can take in, as may well be the case in the second climax of Example 6.6, it tends to filter out what it can't assimilate and to focus on what surfaces as foreground material. Even in much less dense music there may be two or more distinct lines combined in such a sustained way as to require the ear to bounce around from one part to another, trying to pick up enough of each to absorb the full context. Such music has traditionally been called *polyphonic*. Several relationships between its lines are possible:

1. More than one line has independent interest, but one line clearly dominates.
2. All lines are relatively equal, eliminating any foreground-background conflict of interest.
3. Interest shifts as one line then another dominates in an exchange of foreground-background roles.
4. No clear pattern develops.

Examples 6.7–6.10 explore some of these possibilities.

Example **6.7**    Macedonian music
                   *A Young Maiden*

Several types of foreground-background relationships are
evident in this piece for voices, guitar, tupan (a small drum),
and tambourine. The voices are heard first in unison, and then
in a duet in which the two lines are of equal or nearly equal
interest. During the instrumental sections the guitar is clearly
dominant; the percussion instruments form a background.
During the singing the guitar has two different roles: at times
it is roughly equal to the voices in interest, and at other times
it is distinctly subordinate to them.

Q5    During which of the vocal sections—unison or duet—does the
      guitar compete for interest with the voices?
Q6    Which of the two vocal sections creates the most tension? Why?

Example **6.8**    Johann Sebastian Bach
                   *Two-Part Invention No. 8*, 1723

Clearly, the two lines of this piece are independently interesting in their exchange of musical ideas, one line repeating what
the other has just played. This technique is called *imitation*.
At times one line dominates, but then the exchange takes
place and the roles reverse. Sometimes the two lines are
identical in interest. The basic musical material of the beginning
is treated over and over, mostly through imitation, in a very
tight-knit way.

Example **6.9**    Music of Chad
                   *Song to Drive Birds into a Trap*

The two boys sing the same series of melodic formulas, but in
different order. Though the microphone placement for this
recording and differences in voice quality may make one line
seem to dominate, the two parts are of equal interest, and, at
any given moment, highly independent of each other.

Example **6.10**   John McLaughlin
                   *The Love Divine* (excerpt), 1973

Except at the beginning, where the organ is heard alone, no

There are so many delightful things going on in this sixteenth-century Persian miniature that it is hard to know where to look first. It even has two names, The Eavesdropper and The Bathers.

clear pattern of dominance emerges in Example 6.10. Organ, bass, drum-set, guitar, and voices are equally interesting. One reason for this equality is the great activity in each part; another is the fact that each sound source is presented in succession and, once it is heard, remains active, never receding into the background. We are free to float from one part to another, sampling at will.

Get together with two or three friends and, using instruments such as drums, water glasses, saucers, etc., invent a composition with sections that have different foreground-background relationships: a single line dominant, two lines dominant and one supporting, all lines equal. If you use your imagination and stick with it, you will probably make a piece that pleases you.

Listen to one of your favorite pieces and try to observe more foreground-background relationships than you ever noticed before.

Look at some nonrepresentational paintings, studying their foreground-background properties.

## Musical Background

So far we have concentrated on the foreground of two kinds of pieces: those in which a single line dominates, with or without accompaniment, and those with shifting foreground relationships. Now we will turn to the background (or accompaniment) of works in which one line is clearly dominant.

The accompaniment's framework and support for the dominant line can consist of nothing but rhythm, as with drum patterns, or it may be mostly a matter of pitch, often organized as chords. Sometimes rhythm and pitch operate together to form a unified accompaniment, as in Example 6.11.

Example **6.11**    Franz Joseph Haydn
*Symphony No. 94*, second movement (excerpt), 1791

The violins have the dominating melody, while the lower strings play supporting chords, mostly on the pulses of the rather slow two-pulse basic meter. The accompaniment is thus a fusion of rhythm and pitch.

Many times, however, rhythm and pitch are more independent of each other, and it is worth examining them separately in some detail.

*Can you keep your attention fixed on the looming cypress in the foreground, or are you irresistibly drawn to the turbulence of the background sky? (*The Starry Night, *1889, by Vincent Van Gogh)*

### THE RHYTHMIC FACTOR

The most obvious function of rhythm in an accompaniment is to provide a time frame for the dominant material, usually by reinforcing the basic meter while adding activity at other meter levels. Sometimes the interplay of rhythmic patterns is so interesting that it competes with the dominating line. When this happens the accompaniment becomes a source of tension, as we get involved with both accompaniment and melody and try to cope with their combined interest. Rhythmic accompaniment can strongly influence mood or atmosphere by regulating the flow of musical energy (as it did in Example 6.3, for instance).

Examples 6.12 and 6.13 illustrate some of the kinds of interest a rhythmic accompaniment can generate. In Example 6.13 pitch is also a factor, but our attention will be on rhythm.

Example **6.12**    Music of Senufo
            *Drums of the Women*

During the introduction, before the voices enter, the basic
pulse of the piece is marked steadily by the rattles, while low
and high drums break up the faster meter level between them.
The players continue this basic time-keeping faithfully throughout the composition. But the interest goes beyond time-keeping
and support; the total rhythmic vitality of the piece stems
from the liveliness and strength of the percussion accompaniment. Though generally very regular, this accompaniment has a
few deviations that add to its independent interest. Try to
discover where they occur and what makes them different.

Q7    Do these deviations coincide with any particular events in the
       voices?

Example **6.13**    G. Paxton and F. Guilbeau
            *Your Gentle Ways of Loving Me* (excerpt), 1968

This piece gives us a chance to observe a solo and accompaniment in which a variety of rhythmic activity takes place at
four different meter levels:

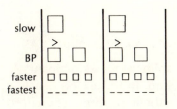

The tempo of the two-pulse basic meter is moderate, marked
most consistently by the bass on the beginning of each pulse.

Q8    On which level does the voice operate? the harmonica? the
       drums?
Q9    Besides marking the basic pulse, the bass sometimes
       uses another level. Which one?

Q10    Following two verses, there is a brief contrasting conclusion. How does the rhythmic activity of the voice and bass change?

Find a songbook that gives accompaniment chords. Play the chords on piano, guitar, or autoharp, in rhythmic patterns as interesting as you can invent. If you don't play an instrument, make up the rhythm patterns and ask a friend to play them.

THE PITCH FACTOR

In Chapter 5 we considered some of the ways in which tonal centers and conventions of pitch relationships are established. These often play an important part in the background role of an accompaniment, as in Examples 6.14–6.19.

Example **6.14**    Music of Kanem
                    *Man's Song with Lute Accompaniment*

This piece employs a drone, one of the simplest and strongest ways to establish a tonal center as a background for other activity.

Q11    Does this drone, like those of bagpipes and tamboura, have more than one pitch?

Example **6.15**    Frédéric Chopin
                    *Piano Sonata No. 2*, Funeral March (excerpt), 1845

From a drone to a chordal accompaniment for a dominant melody can sometimes be a short step. In this excerpt each chord is struck in the simplest of rhythmic patterns: one chord on each pulse of the two-pulse basic meter.

Example **6.16**    Louis Moreau Gottschalk
                    *The Dying Poet* (excerpt), 1864

Nearly as simple rhythmically is the "oom-pah-pah" accompaniment often heard in waltzes with the lowest pitch of the chord on the first pulse of the three-pulse basic meter and the remaining chord pitches on the other two pulses. This pattern is sustained throughout this excerpt.

Example **6.17**   Frédéric Chopin
*Ballade No. 1*, Op. 23 (excerpt), c. 1836

Like Example 6.16, this excerpt is a waltz, with a three-pulse
basic meter.

Q12   Chopin's accompaniment is more subtle than Gottschalk's in
Example 6.16. Why?

Example **6.18**   American music
*My Lord What a Morning* (excerpt)

In the three preceding examples the rhythm of the chordal
accompaniment is extremely simple, with the chords tied to
basic pulses only. Here, although the chords themselves are
less complicated, their pitches are mostly strung out one after
another in more active rhythmic patterns.

In Examples 6.15–6.18 chordal support is generally continuous, but
such support has a different role in *recitative*, a conversational or
narrative element in many vocal works such as operas, oratorios,
and cantatas. The chords accompanying a recitative are usually
played by a keyboard instrument, and most often they punctuate
the nonpulsed rhythm of the vocal line at irregular points in time.

Example **6.19**   Johann Sebastian Bach
*St. Matthew Passion*, "And from the sixth hour"
(excerpt), 1729

In this excerpt two solo voices sing in recitative; the first voice
is that of the Evangelist, who narrates the story, the second
that of Jesus. Chords supporting the words of the Evangelist
are separated by irregular silences, while those supporting the
words of Jesus are sustained. During the chorus sections the
melody is in the top line, supported by chords in the other
voices and by another line that distributes the chord pitches
one after another in a rapid, steady rhythmic pattern.

Example **6.20**   Ukrainian music
*The Maiden from Dunayevtsy*

When the supporting voices are added to the principal melody,
they are layered and locked to the latter's rhythm.

Q13   What effect does the change from one to three voices have on the tension level?

RHYTHM AND PITCH TOGETHER

The final examples of musical background are excerpts from two works in which rhythm and pitch together produce more active and complex accompaniments than we have heard so far.

Example **6.21**   Antonin Dvořák
*Symphony No. 9*, third movement (excerpt), 1893

After the opening unison passage, simple repeated chords in the strings support a fragmented principal melody in the woodwinds. Then the high strings take over the fragmented melody, supported by the winds and mid-range strings in a very active accompaniment. After a second unison passage, the strings play chord pitches one after another in the same rhythmic pattern. Then the full orchestra participates in various active accompaniment figures that support and compete for interest with the original melodic fragments.

Example **6.22**   Gustav Mahler
*The Song of the Earth*, "Drinking Song of Earth's Sorrow" (excerpt), 1908

The accompaniment in the preceding example is fairly complex, but not by comparison with this one, the richness of which is a giant leap from the simple accompaniments heard earlier. So much is going on in pitch structure, rhythmic patterns, and orchestral sounds that the entire accompaniment operates almost independently of the principal vocal line and places great demands on our attention.

Compose two or three melodies using the black keys of the piano. Add different kinds of accompaniment: a drone, a contrasting melody, chords on the black keys.

Do the same thing using all the keys of the piano.

## Synthesis

Nothing could be better than a concerto movement to summarize the ideas of this chapter, as the whole point of a concerto is the interplay of two or more sound sources—sometimes joined, sometimes separated—with a variety of shifting foreground-background relationships as the result. In Example 6.23, the sound sources are two oboes, two clarinets, strings, and harpsichord/bass.

Example **6.23**   Antonio Vivaldi
*Concerto in C Major*, P. 73, first movement, c. 1730

Here, the interplay occurs

1. between the two instruments of one of the pairs of winds
2. between the two pairs of winds
3. between one or both pairs of winds and the group of strings
4. between high- and low-register strings and harpsichord
5. between one or more pairs of winds and low-register strings and harpsichord

In the diagram of the five sections of this movement on page 104, you will see that every section except Section 4 closes with a monophonic unison-octave passage for all instruments. This recurring passage will help you identify the five sections as you listen to the movement.

Midway through Section 1 is a brief passage for oboes and harpsichord/bass only. Immediately before this passage high- and low-register melodies compete for equal attention.

Q14   Does this melodic competition continue immediately *after* this passage?

During Section 2, oboes and clarinets trade places in foreground prominence.

Q15   Is the background of this passage of equal interest to the foreground, or is it less interesting?
Q16   Is the role of the background primarily rhythmic, or is melody an important factor?

FOREGROUND AND BACKGROUND

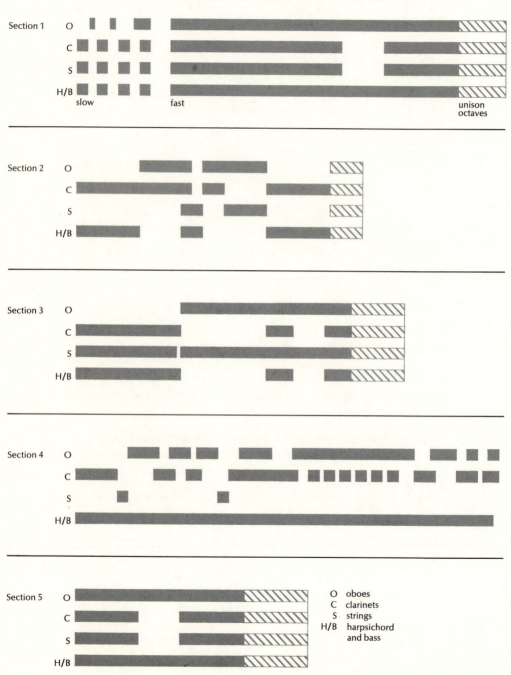

VIVALDI: *CONCERTO IN C MAJOR*, FIRST MOVEMENT—SECTION DIAGRAMS

Section 3 begins with (a) clarinets, low strings, and harpsichord/bass. It continues with (b) oboes against violins; (c) all instruments; (d) oboes against violins again; and (e) all instruments. It closes with the recurring unison-octave passage.

Q17   Prior to this section, the two oboes or the two clarinets always moved together as equals. What new relationship within one of these pairs is set up in (a) above?

Q18   At the beginning of (b), do the oboes and violins exchange material in a way that makes both parts equally interesting?

In Section 4,

Q19   Do the oboe and clarinet pairs mostly alternate or overlap in their foreground role?

Q20   Is the rhythm of the accompaniment generally more active at the beginning than later?

In Section 5,

Q21   Are the foreground-background relationships similar to or different from those of Section 1?

# 7 *Succession and Growth*

Music can be perceived only as it unfolds in time. We can never have a whole musical work in our presence at a single moment as we can a painting. In this respect, a piece of music is more like a piece of sculpture; to sense the sculpture whole we must gather and fuse many perceptions, gained one after another, as the piece is viewed from various angles. This takes time. It is time we can spend as we choose, though—focusing here, concentrating there, secure in the knowledge that the sculpture will not move. But music moves inexorably, never allowing us to study the moment, never pausing for us to catch up. We need quick ears and, often, a good memory to deal with each moment as it goes by.

We can describe *growth* as the outcome of relationships between successive musical events. We might assume that all music is made up of such relationships, but many recent compositions seem to be simply successions of sound events, so that all we need to do is take in what happens as it happens, with little or no need to remember what has gone before or anticipate what may follow.

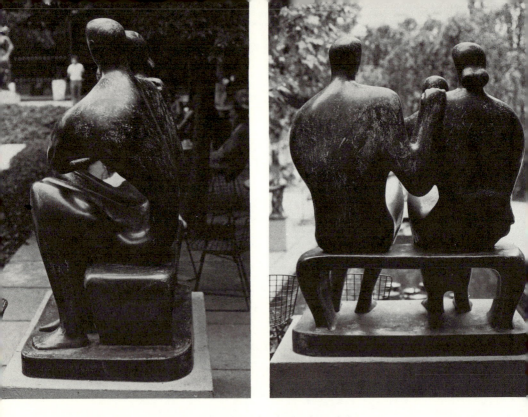

A piece of sculpture shot from the side, the back, and the front in the Museum of Modern Art's Sculpture Garden in New York. (Family Group, 1949, by Henry Moore)

Example **7.1**　John Cage and David Tudor
　　　　　　　*Variations II* (excerpt), 1962

This excerpt is from one version of a piece that could be performed in many very different ways, depending on how the
performer (here, David Tudor) chooses to interpret the very
open-ended directions of the "composer," John Cage. Tudor's
version uses the electronic techniques of amplification and
feedback to alter the sounds the piano can make. Cage says
that such works represent "*dis*organization and a state of mind
which in Zen is called no-mindedness." At most, any relationships between successive sound events seem to be incidental
rather than central to the result.

Although the sound sources and composing-performing manner of
Example 7.1 are contemporary, the idea of unrelated successions
of musical events is not new. In many traditional vocal works music
follows the flow of words in ever-changing ways (as in the recitative
of Example 6.19). And in many improvisatory works—those composed as they are being performed (or designed to sound that
way)—there is often much the same kind of flow of musical ideas
with little interdependence.

Example **7.2**　Johann Sebastian Bach
　　　　　　　*Organ Fantasia in G Minor* (excerpt), c. 1720

Although other parts of this piece are interdependent, this
passage is one of several in which different ideas succeed each
other in improvisatory style, without having much in common.

Much of the music we hear, however, does involve relationships
that we must notice if we are to follow the growth of a composition.
This "art of noticing" requires the same kind of concentration
needed to follow a debate or a lecture; a lapse in attention may
mean losing an important train of thought, with the result that one's
perception of the whole argument is incomplete or flawed.

Following the growth of a piece is like playing a game of expectations—expectations aroused, confirmed, delayed, denied. Here is a visual analogy:

Finding the number 2 in this design is like hearing the first musical event of a composition. With the 2 as a beginning, how will things proceed? Our expectation is that more numbers will follow, although we do not yet know if a design will emerge—that is, if the numbers will be random or ordered. What will the next number be?

Finding that the next number is 4 arouses some expectations and cancels others. Whatever the pattern is to be, it won't be one-after-one: 3 is missing. We still can't tell what the third number will be—6? 8? 7? Perhaps a return to 2? Perhaps a random number that would cancel our growing expectation of a continuing pattern? At this point, the possibilities are narrowing, and the tension of learning the outcome is high.

*Now* we know which possibility has been chosen, and the tension is released by a clear outcome. If, however, the fourth number had been 11 or 17, the firm expectation aroused by 6 would have been denied, the pattern broken, and tension raised to a new level by uncertainty.

No such analogy with music can be exact, but something like this does go on in the growth of compositions that depend on inter-relationships. A composer is constantly generating expectations, then confirming, modifying, delaying, or denying them. In general, the more confirmation, the greater the sense of unity; variety tends to result from modification, delay, or denial. Following the balances between unity and variety in the growth of a piece can become one of the great joys of listening to music, for, as the philosopher R. G. Collingwood has said, to follow the work of a gifted artist is to share the gift. Before turning to a few examples that show how some composers have dealt with the growth of their musical ideas, we will list the four ways (broadly speaking) in which the small bits and pieces that make up those ideas can be treated:

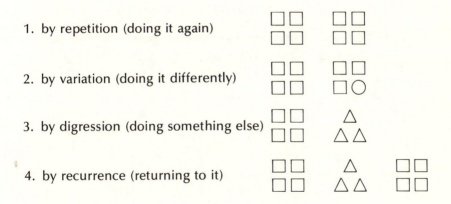

1. by repetition (doing it again)

2. by variation (doing it differently)

3. by digression (doing something else)

4. by recurrence (returning to it)

## Motive, Phrase, Cadence, Section

A *motive* is the smallest germ of musical growth. It is a short, distinctive rhythmic-melodic figure that often forms a part of a longer unit. When first heard, the figure is not a motive, merely an idea. It *becomes* a motive as it is repeated, varied, or returned to as an integrating element.

The *phrase* is the next larger unit of growth. It is a musical idea more or less complete in itself, like a clause in a sentence. Phrases are concluded by *cadences*, endings that are similar to punctuation in writing. A cadence may convey a feeling of completion, functioning like a period at the end of a sentence, or a feeling of momentary pause with more to come, as with a comma. Often two phrases are linked together in a statement-response relationship, the statement ending with an intermediate cadence, the response with a cadence that gives a sense of completion. Often several phrases, in turn, grow into a musical *section*, sometimes complete in itself, sometime open to continuation. If complete, the section may include digression and recurrence in a unity-variety process. Example 7.3 provides a good opportunity to follow the growth of a small musical unit through its use of a motive, its linkage of phrases, and its application of repetition, variation, digression, and recurrence to produce a highly unified yet gently varied whole.

Example **7.3**    Antonin Dvořák
Symphony No. 9, second movement (excerpt), 1893

The rhythmic diagram sets out the slow two-pulse basic meter. It also outlines the actual rhythm of the foreground melody

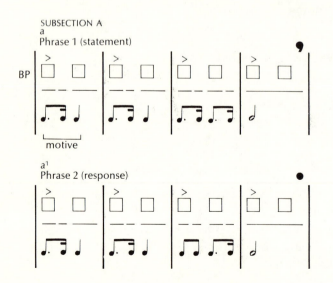

SUBSECTION A
a
Phrase 1 (statement)

motive

a¹
Phrase 2 (response)

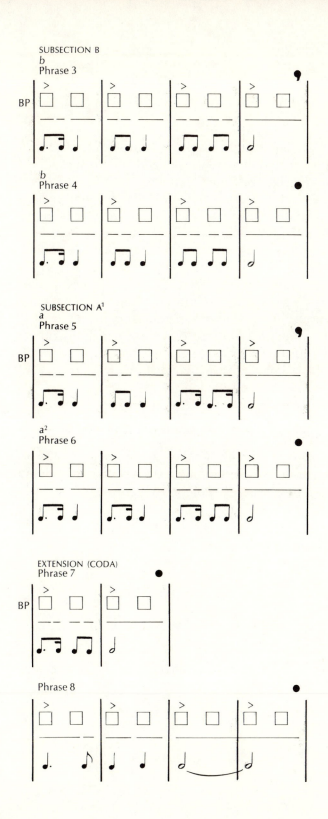

SUBSECTION B
*b*
Phrase 3

*b*
Phrase 4

SUBSECTION A¹
*a*
Phrase 5

*a²*
Phrase 6

EXTENSION (CODA)
Phrase 7

Phrase 8

in proportionate line-lengths (together with pitchless conventional notation, included merely as an additional visual aid). This rhythm, a result of interaction between the basic meter and two faster meter levels, is the key to hearing (and seeing) the repetition and contrast that create unity and variety in the growth of the complete section. The commas and periods show intermediate and conclusive cadences. The cadence ending phrases 1 and 5 is on the dominant; those ending phrases 3 and 4 are on the subdominant. Phrases 2, 6, 7, and 8 end on the tonic. Whenever a small superscript digit follows a letter (such as A[1]), it indicates some kind of variation from the original music (A). It is doubtful that a note-by-note verbal description of all the interrelationships that make up the growth of this section would add much to what you can discover for yourself by close-in, concentrated listening.

In Example 7.4 we turn to a much larger musical unit, a complete symphony movement, to examine the growth process generated from motives and phrases—particularly motives. We will start with five short excerpts, before presenting the whole movement.

Example **7.4**    Ludwig van Beethoven
                  *Symphony No. 7*, fourth movement, 1812

EXCERPT 1

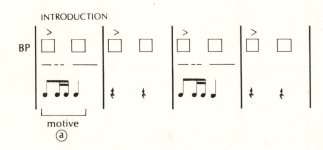

114

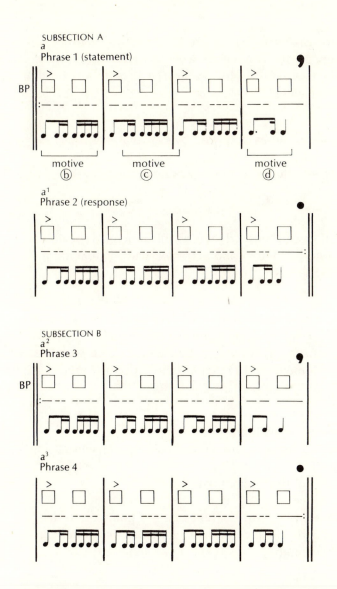

The tight-knit integration of the rhythmic patterns is reinforced by the pitch structure, which keeps repetitions similar throughout. The motives are closely related: the beginning of (b) derives from (a) , as does the whole of (d) , while (c) is a

shift in emphasis from (b) . If you listen to this excerpt care-
fully and repeatedly, you will be well prepared to follow the
further growth from this cell in Excerpts 2–5, and then through
the whole movement.

EXCERPT 2

(a) is stated four times, followed by new material; this much
   is repeated.
(c) is repeated numerous times at various pitch levels.

EXCERPT 3

(a) is stated once.
(b) is stated three times, (d) twice; this much is repeated at
   a different pitch level and extended with several more
   statements of (d).

EXCERPT 4

We now hear a complete statement of Excerpt 1, but at a different pitch level, followed by extensive repetition of (a) and a
brief treatment of (b) with (d); the excerpt closes with the
same two statements of (a) that are the introduction to
Excerpt 1.

EXCERPT 5

(a) is repeated several times.
(c) is repeated a great many times in a long, tension-raising
   passage.
(a) returns as at the beginning of Excerpt 2.

Listen to Excerpts 2–5 several times before going on to discover how much more grows out of Beethoven's small cells in the
complete movement.

COMPLETE MOVEMENT

During the course of the movement you will hear some new,
contrasting passages that do not derive from Excerpt 1.

Q1  Are they as tightly organized as what you heard before?
Q2  Do they grow out of motives, or are they primarily phrase-
    generated?

*Repetition, variation, digression, and recurrence all
contribute to the subtle and intricate growth in this
fourteenth-century Iranian prayer niche.*

Example 7.5 also exhibits considerable growth out of motives.
Although Bartók treats his motives with more variety than Beethoven
does, Bartók produces the same sense of strong cohesiveness.

Example **7.5**   Béla Bartók
*Concerto for Orchestra*, second movement
(excerpt), 1943

The first group of foreground phrases is played by two bassoons,
the second group by two oboes. The motive and phrase material
of the second group contrasts considerably with that of the

*From a single motive—a square—comes the entire growth of this painting. Note how the artist establishes clear foreground-background relationships merely by varying his motive. (Vega, 1957, by Victor Vasarely)*

first. In the first group, the statement-response relationship within each of the two pairs of phrases is much like what we heard in Examples 7.3 and 7.4. Bartók's cadences are not so definitive as in those two examples, but are still quite clear.

Q3   Are phrases equal or unequal in length in the first group? in the second group?

Q4   Which group generates the most tension? (Hint: what was your answer to Q3?)

The two-part character of Example 7.5 derives from closely integrated growth within each section, and a fairly strong contrast between the two sections. Example 7.6 is also in two sections, but this time the two are closely related: the second is a variation of the first. While there are identifiable motives, it is much more the phrase than the motive that is the germ of growth.

Example **7.6**    Duke Ellington
           *Sophisticated Lady* (excerpt), 1940

| *Section 1* | *Section 2* |
|---|---|
| Phrase 1 | Phrase 1 ⎫ variation of |
| Phrase 2: variation of 1 | Phrase 2 ⎬ Section 1 |
| Phrase 3: contrast | Phrase 3 ⎭ |

Q5   Which is the principal means of variation in phrase 2 of Section 1: change of pitch level or change of rhythmic pattern?

Q6   In Section 2 are phrases 1 and 2 more or less elaborate melodically than they are in Section 1?

In Examples 7.4–7.6, growth comes primarily from repetition and variation of motives and phrases. In Example 7.7 we hear a piece that grows out of the repetition of a whole *section*, which is repeated for each verse of the song. This is an ancient way of building an extended piece; you will find it in most ballads, blues, and other folk songs both old and new.

Example **7.7**    American music
           *At the Foot of Yonder's Mountain*

With slight variations, each verse of this Appalachian ballad is sung to the same four-phrase section of music. The similarities in the four phrases link them all in an integrated pattern of growth. At the same time, the differences in the phrases create a three-part structure much like that of Example 7.3: phrases 1 and 2 are closely related as statement and response; phrase 3 provides contrast and heightened tension, while phrase 4 lowers that tension in its similarity to phrases 1 and 2. Unlike Example 7.3, there is an added element of interest—and tension—in that the phrases are less clearly defined, and unequal in length.

Q7   Is the greatest contrast at the beginning or at the end of phrase 3? How is this contrast created?

Q8   Does phrase 4 differ from 1 and 2 mostly in pitch or in rhythm?

Q9   The introduction, interludes between the second and third verses, and conclusion are played on the dulcimer. Are the interludes the same length as the introduction?

119

In Examples 7.3–7.7 rhythm and pitch work together to mark off phrases clearly either by intermediate, on-going cadences, or by cadences with a concluding character. But in much music a more continuous kind of phrase growth results when phrases are elided or overlapped to produce staggered cadences, as in Example 7.8.

Example **7.8.** Leonard Bernstein
*Mass*, "Gospel-Sermon" (excerpt), 1971

This excerpt consists of a brief introduction, verse 1 and refrain ("And it was good"), an instrumental interlude, and verse 2 with the refrain. In the verses, the phrases are elided so that the last word of a solo phrase coincides with the first word of the chorus, and vice versa. In the refrain, the phrases are fully—though very briefly—separated.

Q10  In verse 1, what are the words that coincide on the elisions?
Q11  The instrumental interlude after verse 1 is based on the melody of "And it was good . . . ," but the end of the interlude deviates from the melody. How?

Example **7.9**  Johann Christoph Pezel
*Tower Music*, c. 1680

Each of the two sections of this piece for brasses ends with a strong cadence arrived at simultaneously by all the parts.

Q12  Are there any cadence points common to all the instruments within the first section? within the second?

Example **7.10**  George Crumb
*Ancient Voices of Children*, second movement (excerpt), 1970

Again there are two sections, but this time they are more sharply contrasted, and they have a rather long silence between them. In the first section the oboe plays phrases that cadence independently of those in the mandolin-drums-voice background. The second section begins and ends with the sound of Tibetan prayer stones.

Q13  How does the voice help to create a sense of phrasing?

Using home-made instruments or the black keys of the piano, compose a piece with a pattern of growth like that of one of the examples heard thus far in this chapter.

Using nonsense syllables as your sound source, compose a piece that demonstrates the use of a motive, using the motive to build phrases. Try to modify the motive so that it becomes a new idea. Carry on this process as far as you can make it work.

Form groups of three or four students, each group choosing a piece and analyzing its phrase structure. Present the analyses in class with any visual aids that will clarify them.

## Passage Types

So far we have discussed the growth of a musical composition in terms of the statement, repetition, and variation of motives, phrases, and sections, and digression to introduce contrasting ideas. To control and "map" the growth of a composition as its dimensions increase, composers use a variety of passages that differ in function. Novelists do something very similar—they present their main idea, they vary it (or contrast it) with secondary plots, they bridge from one scene to another in transitional passages, they prepare for the climax of their story, and they round the whole thing off with a conclusion. If you are an attentive reader, you will be aware of the difference in function of all these passages. If you are a careful listener, you will soon be able to identify their musical equivalents, and you will sense how they contribute to the broad span of growth in large-scale compositions. The musical passage types that are easiest to characterize—mostly because of the rhythmic movement typical of each—are presentations, introductions, conclusions, and transitions and/or continuations.

### PRESENTATIONS, INTRODUCTIONS

We have just noted that rhythm is the chief clue to the identification of passage types, that each type tends to have its own way of moving. This is particularly true of *presentation* passages, the category of nearly all the music we have heard in this chapter. Presentations are meant to be *memorable*. They tend to be sharply defined in tune or rhythm—particularly rhythm. Other kinds of passages frame presentations—introducing them, bridging between them, continuing their material, concluding them.

Passages of *introduction* are not restricted to the opening of a work; they may be heard at any point, announcing a presentation. Their character is often static, with little rhythmic interest or forward momentum. This is appropriate, for otherwise they would detract from the ideas they are meant to herald.

Example **7.11**    Miles Davis
*So What* (excerpt), 1961

Example **7.12**    Charles Ives
*The Pond* (excerpt), 1906

Example **7.13**    Don Ellis
*New Horizons* (excerpt), 1968

Each of these examples has an introduction followed by a bit of presentation. Although they differ greatly in style, they all demonstrate clearly the character and function of introduction and presentation.

CONCLUSIONS, TRANSITIONS / CONTINUATIONS

*Conclusion* passages may end a presentation or a transition within a piece, as well as actually finishing it. Rhythmically they are capable of doing two very different things: they can accelerate motion to a climax, or they can slow it down altogether to a halt. Besides rhythm, pitch is often important in conclusion passages because it firmly establishes the tonic in the final cadence. Sometimes composers like to play games, teasing us by making false stops before they *really* conclude.

Example **7.14**    Franz Joseph Haydn
*Symphony No. 101*, second movement
(conclusion), 1794

Example **7.15**    Franz Joseph Haydn
*Symphony No. 104*, fourth movement
(conclusion), 1795

Example **7.16**    Franz Joseph Haydn
*Symphony No. 100*, second movement
(conclusion), 1794

Haydn does something different in each of these three conclusions: in the first he confirms our expectations by gently
slowing to a stop, in the second he passes up several possible
stopping places in a series of mild surprises, while in the third
he foils our expectations completely by turning an apparently
quiet conclusion into an emphatically dramatic one.

The passages hardest to generalize about are those of *transition*
and/or *continuation*. If the function of the passage includes continuation of the presentation, we can get a clue from the similarity
of the musical ideas. In general, though, passages that are mainly
transitional are less defined, less memorable, more mobile and
rambling than those that present, introduce, or conclude. The
difference should be readily apparent in Examples 7.17–7.19. Listen
especially for the tension-producing ambiguity of transitions, as
they lead to the return of the clarity of a presentation.

Example **7.17**    Wolfgang Amadeus Mozart
*Symphony No. 35*, ("Haffner"), K. 385, third movement
(excerpt), 1782

Following (1), a short presentation, comes (2), a not very
memorable continuation-transition consisting mainly of fast-
moving consecutive pitches and little rhythmic definition, then
(3), a second presentation, and (4), a second transition.*

Q14    Is the musical material of (3) different from or the same as (1)?
Q15    (2) and (4), the two transitions, both refer backward and look
forward. Why is this true?

* The numbers correspond to those you'll hear spoken on the recording of Examples
7.17–7.19.

*No lack of clarity at the top or bottom of this woodcut,*
*but look at the ambiguous transitional passage in the center.*
*Fish or fowl? Are you sure? (Sky and Water I, 1938, by M. C.*
*Escher)*

Example **7.18**   Franz Joseph Haydn
             *Symphony No. 16*, first movement (excerpt), c. 1758

This excerpt is similar to Example 7.17, having (1) a presentation, (2) a continuation-transition, and (3) a return to the
presentation.

Q16   The term "presentation" suggests greater musical significance
       than "continuation-transition," but there is an element in (2)
       that contradicts this assumption. What is the element?

Example **7.19**   Felix Mendelssohn
             *Violin Concerto*, first movement (excerpt), 1844

This movement begins with (1) a presentation of the main
musical idea in the solo violin foreground. Then comes (2) a
varied restatement—a second presentation—which flows into

(3) a transition that is much more open-ended and forward-moving than (2), leading to (4) a recurrence of the presentation.

> Listen to several pieces, and sketch an outline showing the function of each identifiable passage.

## Synthesis

Example 7.20 is the kind of piece that seems at first to be a succession of unrelated events. Repeated listenings, however, reveal a well-knit growth.

Example **7.20**    Donald Erb
*Reconnaissance*, second movement, 1967

Listen to the first 60 seconds of the movement, following the diagram on pages 126–27, until you can identify the sound sources: violin, bass, piano, synthesizer, and percussion (vibes, cymbal, and bells). Then listen to the complete movement (recorded separately) as many times as necessary to discover how its recurring sounds tie it together. There are five of these sound-motives, and they act very much like more conventional motives in molding the movement into a coherent whole:

1. slide in pitch
2. sustained or slightly wavering sound
3. trill
4. angular figure
5. chord

Q17   Which pair of motives appears first—3 and 5 or 1 and 2?
Q18   Two motives appear next in quick succession; are they 3 and 4 or 4 and 5?
Q19   Which motive is used more often throughout—3 or 4?
Q20   Which motive is present almost constantly—2 or 5?
Q21   Which motives are brought together tightly to produce a climax at the end?
Q22   In general, what happens to the register as the piece nears its conclusion?

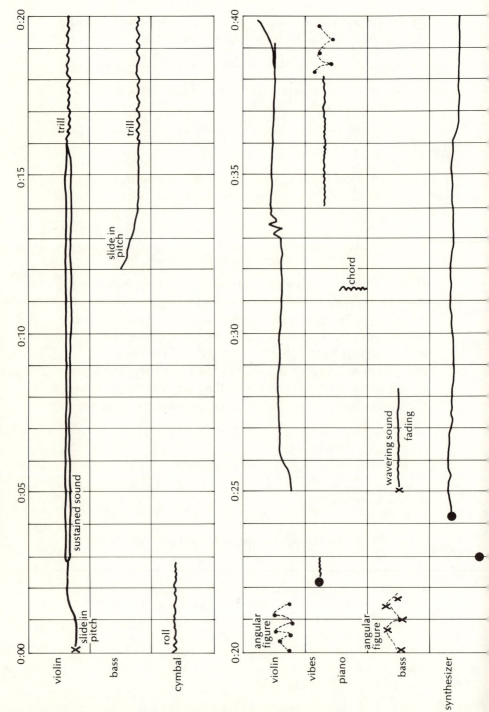

ERB: *RECONNAISSANCE, SECOND MOVEMENT*—DIAGRAM OF FIRST 60 SECONDS

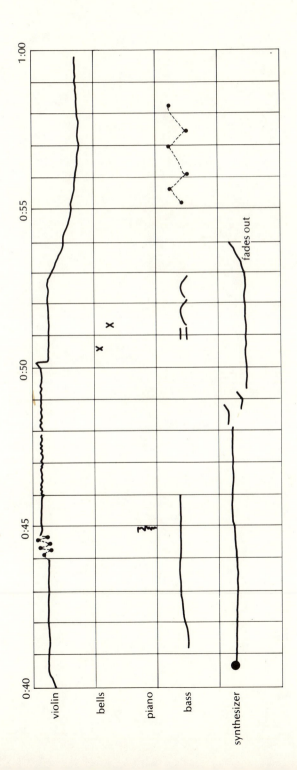

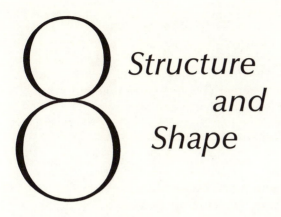

# Structure
# and
# Shape

So far we have been concentrating primarily on individual musical events within a small span of a larger context—on the parts rather than the whole, somewhat as if we had isolated them in a vacuum. But now we turn at last to the composition as a whole, in which these individual events flow together into a total structure and shape.

The *structure* of a composition is its plan of organization, which provides an overall framework for the smaller succession and growth processes we looked at in Chapter 7. In this chapter we will be examining three different kinds of structure:

1. organic structure: a plan of organization that is unique to a particular piece
2. conventional structure: any one of many widely used patterns
3. open structure: a result created by the performer from options offered by the composer

During this chapter we will also be calling your attention to the *shape* of a composition, in which all the small tension-repose effects we have mentioned in earlier chapters come together into a beginning-to-end flow of tension, climax, and repose.

## Organic Structures

A work with an organic structure may be said to have its own growth-determining logic, with its composer allowing its musical events to develop in accordance with their own inherent nature. Such a piece is by no means a succession of unrelated musical events like those of Examples 7.1 and 7.2. Its growth is real and meaningful, with its moments very often related to one another. It might be better to call this kind of structure a *procedure* rather than an organizational plan. Examples 8.1 and 8.2 illustrate this kind of organic procedure.

Example **8.1**　Luciano Berio
*Sinfonia*, Section 4, 1969

Though it follows no traditional pattern, this piece is close-knit and logical; each moment evolves out of what has come before, creating a distinct and unique pattern.

Q1　Several factors contribute to the continuity of this piece. Can you name at least two of them?

Example **8.2**　Johann Sebastian Bach
*Well-Tempered Clavier*, Book 1, Prelude No. 1, 1722

This piece also grows organically, but this time from the single cell heard at the beginning—the pitches of the tonic chord played one after another. Almost a motive, this cell is continuously developed and remains unchanged until near the very end.

Q2　When the change comes, is the length of the pattern expanded or contracted?

*Does the structure of this painting seem arbitrary to you? Do the objects in it seem meaningfully related? The artist named it* Blue Package—*not* Eggs, *or* Paper Bag. *Why? (1971, by Claudio Bravo)*

The device of *imitation* (as in Example 6.8) also tends to produce organic structures. In a very general way, imitation passes a musical idea from one line to another in contexts where there is a good deal of continuous, independent melodic activity in all lines. It may be strict and continuous, as in a round like "Frère Jacques," or as diverse as the several ideas that go from line to line in Example 8.3, an English Renaissance madrigal.

Example **8.3**   Thomas Weelkes
*As Vesta Was from Latmos Hill Descending*, 1601

Q3   For a brief moment, in the middle of the piece, the fairly consistent density is dramatically lightened. What are the words on which this change of density occurs?

Q4   How does Weelkes reflect the sense of the words "came running down amain" in his music for this phrase?

# Conventional Structures

A convention is any method or practice that is in wide enough use to be generally understood and accepted. Among the many possible ways of organizing music, some patterns have proved so useful that they have enjoyed a long life in various guises within our culture, and have thus become conventions. Some belong to other cultures as well. The conventional structures we will discuss in this chapter are *recurrence*, *variation*, and *two-partness*; they are all based on distinctly recognizable *sections* of music, and they are all built on the same principles of repetition, variation, recurrence, and digression that we considered on a small scale in Chapter 7.

RECURRENCE: REFRAIN

Recurrence is a return to something after something else has taken place. Any musical structure based on recurrence must therefore have at least two different sections, one of which acts as a unifying force by recurring after one or more digressions. One of the simplest instances of recurrence is the verse-refrain pattern found so often in work songs and other folk songs. Though the music of all the verses remains the same in such songs, the different words for each verse supply a sense of digression; and the refrain, with the same music and words returning after each verse, supplies a sense of stability—a kind of repeated homecoming.

Example **8.4**    American music
*Will You Miss Me When I'm Gone?* (excerpt)

This excerpt includes:

| Verse 1 | Refrain | Verse 2 | Refrain |
|---------|---------|---------|---------|
| (solo)  | (chorus)| (solo)  | (chorus)|

Q5    Is the second refrain exactly the same as the first, or is it slightly varied?

Example **8.5**    Guillaume Costeley
*Go, Happy Shepherds (Allons, gai gai bergères)*

While Example 8.4 begins with the verse, this sixteenth-century French Christmas song begins with the refrain. This further emphasizes the role of the refrain as a stabilizing element that frames change from beginning to end, as the diagram shows:

| Refrain | Verse 1 | Refrain | Verse 2 | Refrain |
|---------|---------|---------|---------|---------|
| A | B | A | C | A |
| *a b b* | | *b b¹* | | *b b¹* |

| | Verse 3 | Refrain | Verse 4 | Refrain |
|---|---------|---------|---------|---------|
| | D | A | E | A¹ |
| | | *b b¹* | | |

Q6   In what way is the final refrain different from all the others?

Example **8.6**   American music
          *Here, Rattler, Here* (excerpt)

This work song begins with a two-phrase refrain, like a statement and response; each of the phrases is sung first by the soloist, then by the chorus. The rest of the song proceeds with one-line verses, each answered by the first and second phrases of the refrain, in turn:

| Refrain | | Verse 1 (solo) | Refrain (chorus) | Verse 2 (solo) | Refrain (chorus) |
|---------|---|----------------|------------------|----------------|------------------|
| A (solo) | A¹ (chorus) | B | A | B¹ | A¹ |

| | | Verse 3 (solo) | Refrain (chorus) | Verse 4 (solo) | Refrain (chorus) |
|---|---|----------------|------------------|----------------|------------------|
| | | B² | A | B³ | A¹ |

The superscripts with the letters indicate some degree of change in the music; we will use this method throughout this chapter. As indicated, the music of each verse differs somewhat, because of the spontaneous changes improvised by the soloist. These changes heighten the stability of the recurring refrain, despite its own small changes, which the singers of the chorus also supply spontaneously.

## RECURRENCE: RONDO

Many musical structures of varying size and complexity, in works from medieval love songs to contemporary rock, are based on the principle of recurrence in a way similar to the verse-refrain patterns of Examples 8.5 and 8.6: the same music is heard at beginning and end, and between each digression. One of these structures, called *rondo*, has at least two digressions, which differ not only from the recurring section but from each other as well, as in Example 8.7.

>    Example **8.7**   Jean Philippe Rameau
>                     *Musette en rondeau*, 1724

The recurring section of this piece uses a drone, in imitation of the small French bagpipe of the eighteenth century. The overall sectional structure may be outlined as follows:

$$\|{:}\ \underset{a\ a^1}{A}\ {:}\|\ \|{:}\ \underset{b\ b^1}{B}\ \underset{a\ a^1}{A}\ \underset{c\ c^1}{C}\ \underset{a\ a^1}{A}\ \underset{}{D}\ \ \|{:}\ \underset{a\ a^1}{A}\ {:}\|$$

The small letters refer to the two-phrase statement-answer pattern found in each section except D, which is longer and freer. Section D is also a culmination of the progressively greater contrast in Sections B and C. This increasing contrast is the cause of the increasingly greater sense of tension released with each unchanged return of A—one of the effects potentially inherent in any structure with a statement-digression-restatement arrangement.

>    Q7   What does the performer do to provide some variety in the
>          repeated statements within Section A at the beginning and end?

## RECURRENCE: TERNARY DESIGN

In all the preceding examples the recurring section has come back at least twice, following two or more digressions. We come now to a structure having a single return after one contrasting section. Customarily labeled *ternary design*, this structure has been used

ABA¹? No, not really, but the picture certainly has some
sort of ternary design. (Bear in a Tree, undated, by an
unknown American artist)

in a great variety of musical styles, and for pieces ranging in size
from a short folk song to an entire symphonic movement.

Example **8.8**    Hoagy Carmichael
*Georgia on My Mind* (excerpt), 1941

The structure of this tune can be summarized as:

| Introduction | A | B | A¹ |
|---|---|---|---|
| | a a¹ | b | a² |

Q8    In general, one expects the recurrence of a musical idea
following a contrasting section to lower tension by returning to
familiar ground, but in this case tension increases when A¹
begins. Why?

Example **8.9**    John McLaughlin
*Dawn*, 1971

Despite their length and continuity, the three sections of this
ternary structure (ABA¹), should be easy to distinguish. Following the introduction by electric piano, bass guitar, and drums,
A has first a slow melody by violin and guitar, then a guitar
solo that rises and falls in tension, reaching a peak at its end.

This momentum carries into B, which is in a faster tempo; it opens with violin and guitar stating a complex rhythm three times, continues with a violin solo, and closes with the same complex rhythm with which it began. A¹ is a modified return of A; instead of coming to a stop, it simply fades away.

In terms of shape, prolonged tension occurs during the guitar solo and the violin solo; the energy of the complex rhythm adds to the tension, although the rhythm serves to stabilize B by both opening and closing it. A¹ is basically a section of repose, in which the tensions generated earlier are released. The whole tension-repose shape would look something like this:

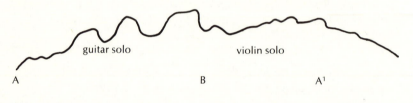

guitar solo              violin solo

A                        B                    A¹

Compose a rhythm piece with a ternary structure, using any handy metal objects. Be sure your basic rhythmic patterns provide enough contrast to distinguish the two different sections clearly.

Improvise an ABACA rondo, using three different sound materials (for example, metal, wood, and glass) for the A, B, and C sections.

RECURRENCE: SONATA FORM

A more complex structure based on the principle of recurrence is *sonata form*, most often found in one or more movements of such multimovement works as sonatas, symphonies, and string quartets. Though sonata form originated in a two-part structure (see page 143), it later took on the three-part structure of ternary design, with these divisions:

| A | B | A¹ |
|---|---|---|
| Exposition | Development | Recapitulation |

Without going into detail about what may happen within any of these divisions—something the very nature of sonata form makes it all but impossible to do—we can abstract a scheme of a sonata-form movement:

| Exposition | | | | Development | Recapitulation |
|---|---|---|---|---|---|
| a | transition | b | close | a and b or other ideas developed | a   transition   b close |
| (original pitch center) | (pitch center changing) | (new pitch center) | | (changes of pitch center) | (usually original pitch center throughout) |

This scheme hints at one of the central features of sonata form: contrast and conflict of pitch centers, with one pitch center (or tonic) solidly established at the beginning and end of the movement and a good deal of change in between, usually reaching a peak in the development section. To follow this pitch-center game often requires rather sophisticated listening ability. Here we note only that the game exists, and that learning to follow it is very rewarding.

The observations below about the three divisions of a sonata-form movement are necessarily as general as the scheme above, but they may be helpful by way of background before you listen to a complete sonata-form movement in Example 8.10.

1. *Exposition*. One or more strongly marked (and often contrasted) musical ideas are presented here, sometimes preceded by an introduction, sometimes not. A new pitch center is usually in force from the presentation of the second main idea through the end of the exposition. During the exposition one or more transitional passages appear, which are different in nature from the presentational quality of the main ideas, as is the closing passage. Even before the development section proper, these transitional and closing passages may develop the main ideas by fragmenting, expanding, or otherwise varying them. Often, the entire exposition section will be repeated.

2. *Development*. This section is the arena for the pitch-center

game mentioned earlier. The development often opens with the same pitch center that was established at the end of the exposition and closes on the dominant of the original pitch center, in preparation for the recapitulation. The materials of the development consist of at least one of the main ideas—or sometimes just one or more motives—that were presented in the exposition. No other generalizations about the development section are possible. There is no end to the number of ways in which musical ideas can be manipulated or new pitch centers introduced. By definition, the development section is full of surprises, and it is there-fore, of course, the greatest source of tension in the movement.

3. *Recapitulation*. This section more or less straightforwardly repeats the materials of the exposition, although it usually hovers around the original pitch center throughout. This single pitch center is necessary here to lower the tension of the development section and to insure stability and repose for the end of the movement. The recapitulation may or may not be followed by a coda, a concluding passage with the paradoxical function of providing a suffix of continuing vitality at the end of the movement while it winds it down completely.

Example **8.10**    Wolfgang Amadeus Mozart
*Symphony No. 38* ("Prague"), K. 504
third movement, 1786

Listen to the movement several times, noting the divisions as they are announced on the recording. When you are familiar with it, try the following questions:

Q9    During the exposition, does the transition
    a. glide smoothly from *a* to *b* without a break?
    b. interrupt for a new idea?
    c. interrupt for a further treatment of *a*?

Q10    By comparison with *a*, is *b*
    a. more aggressive?
    b. less aggressive?
    c. initially more gentle and then more aggressive?

Q11    Is the close of the exposition
       a. closely related to *b*?
       b. entirely new?
       c. closely related to *a*?
Q12    Is the material treated in the development
       a. derived solely from *a*?
       b. derived solely from *b*?
       c. related to both *a* and *b*?

> Listen to the first movements of any two symphonies by Haydn or Mozart. Devise some kind of graph or verbal description that will help you recognize the similarities or differences in the way sonata form is treated.

## VARIATIONS

In Chapter 7 we mentioned the principle of variation as one of the four basic ways in which composers treat their musical ideas during the growth of a composition. This kind of variation of details can be found in nearly all musical structures in all cultures. Now, though, we are talking about variation as a musical structure in its own right, in which a clearly defined musical unit—a small section, a complete tune, a fixed set of chords, for example—is presented and then systematically varied a number of times to produce an entire movement or work, with each variation forming a part of the whole. In western culture this procedure goes back at least as far as the Middle Ages, when repetitions of a tune were often enhanced by improvised variations of it.

Example **8.11**     Anonymous
                        *Chansonetta tedesca*

This "little German song" of the fourteenth century is performed on the shawm with an accompaniment of medieval fiddle and drums. Following the drone-and-drum introduction the shawm plays the tune in plain fashion. Then, after a brief fiddle-and-drum interlude, it plays a variation of the tune.

From the sixteenth century to our own time, sets of variations on a theme—often a popular tune—have been written in many styles but with essentially the same structural plan. We will examine one such set in some detail.

Example **8.12**    Franz Schubert
*Piano Quintet* ("Trout"), fourth movement, c. 1819

Schubert took the theme of this movement from his song "The Trout," and wrote a set of six variations on it for piano, violin, viola, cello, and bass. The structure of the theme is a small ternary form:

$$\|: a \;\; a^1 :\| \; b \; \|: a^2 :\|$$

This form is retained in each variation, all of which are self-contained, except for the link between Variations 5 and 6. Every variation puts the theme in a new context.

*Variation 1:* The piano ornaments the theme, the bass plays a pizzicato (plucked) line, and the other three strings play short, darting figures, sometimes imitating the piano trills.

Q13    Does the piano play anything besides the ornamented melody?

*Variation 2:* The cello plays the melody, imitated by the piano. The high violin part is a very active, decorative melody moving at a faster pace than the other instruments.

Q14    Does the bass play an independent melody or simply support by playing a part of the background chords?

*Variation 3:* The bass plays the theme, joined by the cello at a couple of phrase ends, while the piano takes over the brilliant decorative melodic role the violin had in Variation 2. Its strength almost overshadows the theme.

Q15    Do the violin and viola play a rhythmic or a melodic role?

*Variation 4:* There is an abrupt shift in mood and in treatment of the theme. Both the bold chords at the beginning and the lighter, active interplay later almost completely obscure the theme itself.

Q16    Does the bass play a sustained line or is it strongly active on nearly every pulse?

*Variation 5:* The cello solo is once again clearly related to the theme, though considerably changed as compared with Variations 2 and 3. In the second part of the variation the pitch center moves far from the original tonic; for this reason the extension is needed to get back to the tonic for the final variation.

*Variation 6:* The theme returns in a plain, undecorated version, with an accompaniment that brings back the darting figures of Variation 1. The original structure is stretched out by repeating the *b* and *a*² portions, which are followed by a brief concluding extension.

Q17    Which two instruments share the theme?
Q18    Which two instruments exchange the darting figure?

The shape of the whole set of variations is reasonably clear: a low-level beginning with the simple theme, a heightened level of similar activity in Variations 1 and 2, that level raised higher with the brilliance of Variation 3, a peak of tension in the opening of Variation 4, and then a slow relaxation toward the repose of the theme's simplicity in Variation 6:

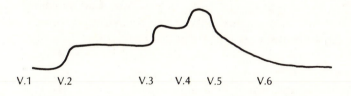

V.1      V.2              V.3    V.4    V.5        V.6

There are many pieces of older music in which the relationship of one or more variations to the original theme is much more remote than in Example 8.12. This is also true of Example 8.13, a con-

*A wedding quilt, made in 1876 and found in Vermont.*
*If the scene in the center is the theme, what are the twelve*
*outer sections?*

temporary piece. Each of its variations has its own distinguishing character, but specific associations with the theme range from moderately close to quite distant.

Example **8.13**   Walter Carlos
    *Variations for Flute and Electronic Sounds*, 1964

Following the presentation of the flute melody (the theme) are six variations:

*Variation 1:* Flute and electronic sounds, independent of each other.

*Variation 2:* The flute begins alone, followed by two electronic parts in imitation. The flute finishes alone.

*Variation 3:* Electronic sounds only.

*Variation 4:* A flute solo with one bit of electronic punctuation.

*Variation 5:* Close interchange between flute and electronic sounds, with much trilling.

*Variation 6:* Flute and electronic sounds, largely independent of each other as in Variation 1; a dramatic summation.

Q19  What happens to the original material in the first variation?

Example 8.13 represents a rather specialized twentieth-century use of the variation structure, but the structure has been widely used in more conventional ways in our time. Most of jazz, nearly all instrumental blues, and many rock pieces have developed out of variations on a tune, a set of chords, or a repeated bass.

Compose a theme and variations using spoken sounds only. Construct the theme from a pattern of words. Develop variations by modifying the sounds of the words, changing the word order, using contrasting vocal sounds, or adding a percussion accompaniment.

TWO-PARTNESS

The third structural pattern that has been used widely enough to be regarded as a convention is the division of a piece into two distinct parts. The relationship between the two parts can be one of sharp contrast or one of close-knit continuity of shared materials, with any number of shadings between these extremes. Examples 8.14–8.17 provide a small sampling of the possibilities.

Example **8.14**   Henry Purcell
*Dido and Aeneas*, Overture, 1689

The distinction in mood and character between the two parts of this work is clearly marked—the first part slow and serious,

*The eighteenth-century Connecticut gravestone of four young brothers. Do you see a parallel between its structural pattern and one of the musical structures discussed in this chapter?*

the second much livelier. Each section grows in seamless fashion out of its own single basic idea. The first section is not repeated, the second is; here is the overall structure:

A ‖: B :‖

**Example 8.15**    South Indian music
*Raghuvāranannu* (excerpt)

The excerpt presents only the conclusion of the first part of this vocal work and the beginning of what follows. As in Example 8.14, the contrast between the two parts is very marked; the opening section moves in a leisurely way, with brief melodic bursts in a freely rhythmic manner. As the second section begins, the *mridangam* (drum) enters, the rhythm becomes strongly pulsed, the pace quickens, the voice and violin figures are more sharply defined, and the whole takes on a sense of urgent forward propulsion.

Many pieces of the seventeenth and eighteenth centuries—including innumerable dance pieces—are in two parts with each part repeated. In some, the musical materials of the two parts differ:

‖: A :‖: B :‖

In many others the two sections share the same materials:

‖: A :‖: A¹ :‖

In both cases the two-partness is emphasized by strong cadences at the end of each section and by the repetition of each section.

Example **8.16**   William Byrd
*Lord Salisbury's Pavan*, c. 1600

In this dance (intended more for listening than for dancing) each section has different musical material. The performer provides some variety in the repetitions by changing the sound of the harpsichord.

Example **8.17**   George Frideric Handel
*Flute Sonata*, Op. 1, No. 11, second movement, 1731

The two sections of this movement share the same musical ideas. Each section begins with the same figure, followed by a few short phrases, and concludes with a much longer and more active phrase. The shape can be shown like this:

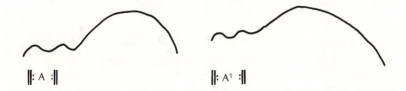

‖: A :‖                                          ‖: A¹ :‖

MIXED STRUCTURES

Within a single piece, composers often use more than one of the conventional structures we have been examining. The different kinds of two-partness we saw in Examples 8.16 and 8.17, for instance, came to be modified by the principle of recurrence, producing a combination of two- and three-partness called *rounded binary*, the source of sonata form. Two of the possible rounded binary schemes are

A   A¹             A   B

‖: *a* :‖: *a¹ a* :‖    or    ‖: *a* :‖: *b a¹* :‖

Example **8.18**   Wolfgang Amadeus Mozart
*Symphony No. 35* ("Haffner"), K. 385
third movement, 1782

In the diagram of this movement below, the capital letters show the overall ternary design, and the small letters show the two-part substructures within it. (The diagram is incomplete; you will complete it yourself when you answer Q20.)

A   A¹   B        A A¹

‖: *a* :‖: *a¹a* :‖: *b* :‖: ? ? :‖ *a a¹a* ‖

Each of the main sections A and B is a separate minuet, one of the most common eighteenth-century dances. At the time this movement was composed, it was customary to repeat the final *a* and *a¹-a* sections. Present-day performances eliminate this repetition, however, so that the two-partness of this final section disappears.

Q20   Which scheme represents the missing small letters in the B section: *c-b*, or *b¹-b*?

Example 8.18 has a rather simple mixture of two structural patterns, but the mixture in Example 8.19 is considerably more intricate.

Example **8.19**   Franz Joseph Haydn
*Piano Sonata*, H. 43, third movement, c. 1773

The main sections form a clear rondo—ABACADA—and you may want to listen first for this plan of digression-recurrence. To aid you, each section is announced as it begins.

You may have discovered in listening that no two of the recurrences of A are quite alike. Each is varied, but not simply and straightforwardly as in the Schubert quintet movement

146

(Example 8.12). The following outline is complex, but if you will stay with it while listening to the movement several times, you will hear some of the subtleties a skilled composer can bring to bear in fusing three structural conventions: rondo, variations, and ternary design.

| A | | B | A¹ | | C | A² | | D | A³ | | Coda |
|---|---|---|---|---|---|---|---|---|---|---|---|
| $a\,a^1 b\,a\,a^1$ | | | $a\,a^1 \begin{Bmatrix} a\,a^1 b\,a\,a^1 \\ \text{variation 1} \end{Bmatrix}$ | | | $\begin{Bmatrix} a\,a^1 b\,a\,a^1 \\ \text{variation 2} \end{Bmatrix}$ | | | $a\,a^1 \begin{Bmatrix} a\,a^1 b\,a\,a^1 \\ \text{variation 3} \end{Bmatrix}$ | | |

A few more comments may help:

1. In A, *a* and *a*¹ are two short phrases in a statement-response relationship.
2. In A¹ Haydn begins with an exact recurrence of *a-a*¹, leading us to expect an unchanged return to A before denying that expectation by launching into a variant.
3. In A² variation is begun at once, with no expectation of exact return.
4. A³ begins with the identical pitches of A and A¹ but shifts to a lower register, referring subtly to the beginning of B, which started in the same way.

The shape of the piece is closely related to the sectional structure. Within A there is a small rise and fall of tension in the statement and response of *a-a*¹, while the length and contrast of *b* raise more tension, released by the return to *a-a*¹. Section B has considerable change; consequently, its level of tension increases.

Q21    What effects of tension or repose does A¹ bring into play?

Section C reaches the highest point of tension with more contrast than anything that has come before.

Q22    How does A² compare with A¹ in tension-repose effect?

Section D starts out as a conclusion, but the surprise of its continuation provides new impetus and a fresh source of tension, released finally by the concluding recurrence of A³ and the brief coda.

## Open Structures

All the preceding examples in this chapter have come to the moment of performance in some pre-established form, and whatever changes occur from one performance to another are matters of detail—different interpretations of how the composer intended the written notes of a composition to sound, or improvised contributions that are part of a given style, such as jazz. But the fundamental structure of them all remains the same, time after time. Not so with many pieces of our own time, in which composers ask performers to make choices that guarantee the piece will never be performed in exactly the same way twice. This process allows for possibilities that would probably not have occurred to the composer; but even if they had—a highly unlikely situation—the composer could not have notated them exactly. Such pieces are something like mobiles; their materials are meant to be open to constantly shifting relationships. Some offer the performer(s) only a narrow set of choices, while others present an almost unlimited invitation to improvise. Example 8.20 illustrates not *the* structure and shape of Earle Brown's piece, but one possible version that resulted from one particular set of choices made on one particular occasion. The performance you will hear is a once-only event.

Example **8.20**   Earle Brown
*Piece for Any Number of Anythings* (excerpt), 1970

Brown's "score" (opposite) describes five kinds of activity, each of which is improvised by the performers. A conductor (in this recording, Brown) makes the necessary choices: which activity will come when, how long it will last, how loud it will be, etc.

Get a group of fellow students or friends together and perform this piece. Use instruments or voices; take turns at conducting, making sure that whatever signals you need to use for start-stop, loud-soft, and fast-slow are simple and clear. Be imaginative and try for interesting outcomes.

SCORE BY EARLE BROWN FOR HIS *PIECE FOR ANY NUMBER OF ANYTHINGS*

| 1 | 2 | 3 | 4 | 5 |
|---|---|---|---|---|
| long high notes | quick angular melodic lines | very legato lines | highly fragmented lines | very small noisy sounds on instruments* |
| slowly changing melodic lines | abrupt dynamic changes (normal sounds but vary timbre*—pizzi- cato, arco, etc.) | note-to-note intervals <u>no more than a</u> perfect fifth | note-to-note intervals always <u>more than one octave!</u> | * Timbral condi- tions may be translated into comparable or similar sounds from voices. |
| small intervals | vary durations | | | |

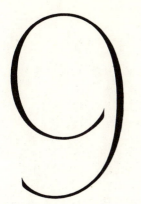

# Tension
## and Repose:
## A Summary

In Chapters 1–7 we often asked you to notice specific details in terms of their capacity to generate tension and repose, and in Chapter 8 we noted how cycles of tension and repose determine the shape of a composition. Because tension and repose cycles result from an intricate cause-and-effect network, they are elusive. Because they are at the center of our response to music, it is well worth devoting this final chapter to them.

## Conditioning and Attitude

Tension and repose cycles work on two levels. The simpler level is the effect of a sound wave on the human eardrum and nervous system. On this level the response of any group of listeners who share the same cultural conditioning will probably be similar: an extreme of any kind will increase tension, and moderation of that extreme will decrease it. Loud and soft are one pair of extremes— the intensity of high amplification or the hush of a barely audible sound. Other pairs are slow and fast; high and low; complex and simple—more information than the ear can take in or less than it can tolerate. A more subtle pair of extremes is great or little change

*One kind of tension-generating extreme—too much information.*
*(University Boulevard, Denver, Colorado)*

within any of the other pairs. There are no absolutes—tension and repose are always relative—and there are individual differences, of course, in degree of response. But in talking about extremes and their moderation, we can be reasonably sure that there will be more similarity than difference in their tension-repose impact on any group of listeners with a culture in common.

> Find a few pieces that involve some of the extremes mentioned. Share them with friends who are not studying music and test our assumption of common cultural response.

The second level—the one that most concerns us—is much more subtle, complex, and personal. We can express it as an equation:

music × (perception + attitude) = tension-repose response

The unknown variable in this equation is *you*. The more involved your attitude and the sharper your perception, the larger your musical "product" will be.

## Sources of Tension and Repose

By way of preface to the musical examples in this chapter, try the following experiments:

1. Strike or pluck a single sound on a piano (hold the key down), guitar, violin, vibraharp, gong, or similar instrument. Listen to the sound until it disappears completely. Which part of this experience is tension? Which part is repose?
2. Use the same sound source, but this time ask a friend to produce the sound. As it starts, clench your fist and take a deep breath. As it decays, slowly open your hand and exhale. This should help suggest how it is possible to become intimately wrapped up in a tension-repose cycle of sound.
3. Finally, still using the same sound source, turn your back to it. Ask your friend to play the sound for you several times at irregular intervals over a span of three to five minutes, responding as you did in the preceding experiment. What new variable affects your perception of tension and repose?

Though these exercises are elementary, they should demonstrate that even the simplest acoustical phenomenon—the single sound—is a source of tension and repose.

> By yourself or with one or more members of your class, perform John Cage's 4'33". Be sure to perform the entire work! After the performance consider this question: where is the tension and where is the repose?

### EXPECTATION AND SURPRISE

From all the preceding experiences you will probably have discovered that two of the most potent sources of tension are ambiguity and the unexpected. Conversely, clarity and the appearance of the expected are sources of repose. The question is, what is the expected? What makes a moment ambiguous? The answer lies in our conditioning—once we have enough experience with the kind of music at hand, we will know its probabilities or possibilities, and we will recognize a surprise when it comes. Examples 9.1–9.5 will help to illustrate expectation and surprise.

Example **9.1**   Flamenco music
              *Alegrias* (excerpt)

The extraordinary length, intensity, and high range of the opening vocal passage fly in the face of "normal" expectation and create a high level of tension—probably due in part to the listener's almost physical identification with the singer's effort. The short phrases following seem more customary in length and effort, and thus provide a measure of repose.

Q1   Does the concluding vocal passage further relax the tension or raise it to a new level?

Example **9.2**   Johann Sebastian Bach
              *Brandenburg Concerto No. 4*, first movement
              (excerpt), 1721

In this work, as in Example 9.1, tension is generated through unexpected length. The piece opens with two balancing phrases of equal length, each lasting for six three-pulse basic-meter groups. This phrase pair is followed by an unpredictably long unbroken phrase, which lasts for *ten* three-pulse groups. This phrase raises the tension considerably. Then the first two balancing phrases return with the kind of stabilizing, repose-generating effect characteristic of any recurrence after contrast.

Q2   Do you expect that the phrase that follows this recurrence will again be long and unbalanced? Is it?
Q3   Is this phrase longer or shorter than the ten-group phrase?
Q4   What effect does the length of this phrase have on tension?

Example **9.3**   Wolfgang Amadeus Mozart
              *Variations on "Ah, vous dirai-je, Maman"* (theme), 1778

This is the same tune as "Twinkle, Twinkle Little Star." The pitches for those four words form the first part of a two-part phrase. They create tension by raising certain expectations: that the second part will be equal in length to the first; that the rising pitches of the first part will be answered by descending pitches in the second; and that the second part will return to the tonic pitch, with which the first began. All these expectations are fulfilled, and a small tension-repose cycle is completed.

Q5  The two-part phrase described above is immediately repeated. Does this raise or lower tension? Why?

Q6  After this repetition, a contrasting two-part phrase is introduced. The second part of this new phrase is a slightly varied repetition of the first part. What tension-repose effects are provided by the slight variation?

Q7  What effect does the concluding phrase of the theme have?

Example **9.4**  Ernst von Dohnányi
*Variations on a Nursery Song* (theme), 1913

This is another version of the tune in Example 9.3. The difference between the two reveals a little more about expectation and surprise and their tension-repose impact. It also illustrates a point we mentioned earlier: the more musical information the listener must take in, the greater the tension generated. With this in mind, compare the first statement of the first two-part phrase in each version. It is obvious that the Mozart has more information—a foreground melody and a background accompaniment. The Dohnányi has only the melody, doubled at the octave.

Q8  Which version has more new information, and therefore more tension, in the repetition of the first phrase?

Now compare the contrasting two-part phrase in each version, and the return to the opening phrase of each.

Q 9  Which version creates more tension? Why?

Q10  Are there any tension-creating surprises in the Dohnányi that the Mozart lacks?

Example **9.5**  Wolfgang Amadeus Mozart
*String Quintet*, K. 515, second movement (excerpt), 1787

In this piece Mozart plays a quite sophisticated game of expectations. The structural outline below shows the basic ternary plan. Unlike most such designs, however, every phrase is derived from the very first one; hence all the a's, with each numeral indicating a new variant.

$$A \quad | \quad B \quad \quad A^1$$
$$\mathbf{\|:}\ a\ a^1\ \mathbf{:\|}\ \ a^2\ a^3\ a^4\ \ \ a^5\ a^6\ a^7\ a^8$$

Throughout, the continuing presence of the opening phrase is a stabilizing factor, tending toward repose. Except for the tension-lowering effect of the immediate repetition of $a$-$a^1$, however, this stability is more than counterbalanced by unpredictable changes that make each phrase different in some significant way from all the others.

Q11   Like most listeners, you very likely expect phrase $a$ to be answered by a phrase of equal length. How does Mozart raise the tension by denying your expectation?

Q12   Phrases $a^2$ and $a^3$ are related to $a$ and $a^1$. How does the length of $a^3$ raise the tension further?

Q13   Phrases $a^5$ and $a^6$ are a recurrence of $a$ and $a^1$, with the same length relationship. What changes prevent them from providing the repose of an exact recurrence?

Q14   What expectation aroused by $a$ and denied by $a^1$ is finally fulfilled by $a^7$ and $a^8$?

Q15   Which phrase reaches the highest level of tension because of the complexity of its contents—the number of things to take in simultaneously?

REPETITION

Examples 9.1–9.5 have used repetition or recurrence in ways that provided stability and, thus, relative repose. But repetition can produce the opposite effect, too. If it is insistent—if it is carried past a listener's own point of tolerance—it can be a source of unbearable tension. In an Indian raga, for example, the constant repetition of the tonic by the drone of the tamboura—sometimes for an hour or more—can have one of two effects: it can drive an unattuned listener right up the wall, or it can provide an ultimate

*A still from the Nikolais Dance Theatre's production of*
*"Tensile Involvement." The choreographer's notes indicate the*
*position of the weights necessary to produce maximum tension*
*in both the broad bands of elastic and the dancers' bodies.*

sense of repose if the listener has come to terms with the
nature of the music.

Example **9.6**    Terry Riley
            *In C* (excerpt), 1964

Though vastly different from the drone of an Indian raga,
insistent repetition is the core of this work. The excerpt is a
brief portion of a piece that can go on in this manner for forty-
five to ninety minutes, as determined by the performers. How do
you respond to it? Does the tension of repetition drive you out
of the experience within a few seconds? Is the excerpt long
enough for you to be liberated from the tension and relax into
the curious effect of a kind of zero gravity?

Examples 9.7 and 9.8 use repetition in more involved or more
ambiguous ways than *In C*, now generating, now releasing tension.

157

Example **9.7**   Mick Jagger
                *Silver Train* (excerpt), 1973

An ostinato figure on the tonic chord begins this piece and is repeated many times, building up considerable tension. In fact, no change occurs for almost a full minute. When the dominant chord arrives we are momentarily released from the tension of the insistent tonic, but then another build-up of tension begins that does not subside until the original ostinato *returns* toward the end of the excerpt. Do you hear the piece this way?

Example **9.8**   Igor Stravinsky
                *The Rite of Spring*, "Dance of the Adolescents"
                (excerpt), 1913

Like most introductions, the brief introductory passage in this excerpt raises some tension in anticipation of what is to follow. A stabilizing element is then established—a clocklike pulse, on which there is shortly superimposed a driving rhythm with unpredictably erratic pulse groups. This passage, dramatic and tension-filled, drops out, returns, drops out again, returns again. Though never quite the same, its recurrences become a stable factor, gradually changing the impact of the passage from high tension to moderate repose.

The tension-repose cycles of Examples 9.1–9.8, though very different in size and in degree of impact, all result from surprises sprung, and expectations aroused that are denied or fulfilled. But Example 9.9 is another matter altogether.

Example **9.9**   Robert Ashley
                *She Was a Visitor* (excerpt), 1966

No amount of experience with more conventional music is likely to help you in a piece like this. When you first hear it, you may not be able to sense any predictability or any source of repose—only the perpetual tension of a continuous stream of musical moments in constant change behind the insistently repeated foreground words. But continuity and a measure of repose are here, and you will find it rewarding to listen to the piece until you can sense its own unique flow of tension raised and lowered.

Choose a recording at random and try to discover its sources of tension and repose. List all the ways you can think of in which tension is generated.

Listen to your favorite piece of music and do the same thing.

Listen to your instructor's favorite piece of music and do the same thing.

OTHER SOURCES

Examples 9.10–9.13 illustrate several other sources of tension-repose cycles—provided one notices them.

Example **9.10**    Béla Bartók
    *Concerto for Orchestra*, fifth movement (excerpt), 1943

This excerpt is in six sections:

1. a fanfare-like passage for brasses
2. a long, active passage primarily for strings
3. a simpler passage for full orchestra, with some broad gestures
4. the same kind of activity as in Section 2, with fuller instrumentation
5. the gestures of Section 3, extended
6. a simple tune played by woodwinds, supported by strings and triangle

Q16    Why does the sustained sound in Section 1 create tension?
Q17    What factors contribute to rising tension in Section 2?
Q18    Does Section 3 provide more or less tension than Section 2? Why?
Q19    How does Section 4 create both repose and tension in relation to what has gone before?

Q20 Sections 3 and 5 begin similarly. Which reaches a higher level of tension? How?

Q21 Does Section 6 bring more repose or greater tension? Why?

Example **9.11**   Iannis Xenakis
*Akrata* (excerpt), 1965

This excerpt uses three kinds of brass sounds: rapidly tongued pitches, sustained straight tones, and (later) the rough growl of flutter-tonguing.

Q22 Describe three things that increase tension in this excerpt and three that decrease it.

Example **9.12**   Mort Dixon and Ray Henderson
*Bye Bye Blackbird* (excerpt), 1956

Example **9.13**   Dixon and Henderson
*Bye Bye Blackbird* (excerpt)

Example 9.12 is from the the record *Round About Midnight* by the Miles Davis Quintet; Example 9.13 is from *Miles Davis in Person*. A comparison of these two versions of the same song, played by the same principal artist, shows what differences in tension level can be created by two interpretations. The tune may be outlined as follows:

Introduction   phrase *a*   phrase *a*¹   phrase *b*   phrase *a*²

Q23 Which version strikes you as the simpler, more straightforward presentation of the tune?

Q24 What overall factors in 9.13 create a level of tension somewhat higher than the level in 9.12?

Q25 Which introduction has a greater measure of tension? Why?

Q26 Compare phrase *a* in the two versions. What surprise raises the tension in 9.13? How does this same thing *lower* tension in phrase *a*¹ of 9.13?

Q27 Why do phrases *b* and *a*² of 9.13 have a higher tension level than the same phrases in 9.12?

*Does the tension level of this painting seem very high to you or very low? Are any of the ideas in this chapter helpful in making or explaining your choice? (The Whitestone Bridge, 1939, by Ralston Crawford)*

*The young conductor Kazuyoshi Akiyama in tension . . .*

> Invent any device, gadget, or project—no matter how farfetched
> —that convinces you personally of the validity of the ideas in this
> chapter.

The end of this book merely marks a beginning. Music is a vast
and continually expanding art that resists any effort to "explain" it

*. . . and in repose.*

or freeze it in words. Its logic is *musical*, not verbal. In your day-to-day listening you will encounter much music that relates to the topics in this book. You will also encounter much that does not. But in the latter case, you will not be at a loss if you have succeeded in opening your ears and sharpening your intuition. After all, listening to music is ultimately a matter of intuition. It is also one of life's most personal and enriching experiences.

# Answers

# 1

Example **1.26**

Q1    Line 6.      Q2     Four times.

Q3    The diamond marimba and chromelodeon.

Q4    The kithara.      Q5     Three.

# 2

Example **2.4**

Q1    The level of tension drops off sharply.

Q2    Immediately.

Example **2.5**

Q3    There are two major increases, both gradual.

Q4    The pace decreases.

Example **2.9**

Q5    Accelerando (though within a very brief time span).

Q6    Before the second section.

Example **2.10**

Q7    The second.      Q8     With a gradual ritardando.

Q9    Yes, by creating a sense of anticipation.

Example **2.11**

Q10    Rubato is used throughout.

Example **2.12**

Q11 Abrupt.

Q12 First there is a ritardando, used to slow down the pace and complete the idea; then there is an abrupt shift to a faster tempo, creating something like an exclamation.

Example **2.13**

Q13 Lines 6, 7, 8, and 9.     Q14 "Ah!"

Q15 "del," "qui," "saro."     Q16 Line 6.

Q17 It increases.     Q18 Line 13.     Q19 Faster.

Q20 Line 13

# 3

Example **3.3**

Q1 Moderately fast.     Q2 Threes.     Q3 Threes.

Example **3.4**

Q1 Fast.     Q2 Twos.     Q3 Threes.

Example **3.5**

Q1 Moderate.     Q2 Twos.     Q3 Twos.

Example **3.21**

Q4 Twos.     Q5 A steady stream of twos.     Q6 Slower.

Q7 They mostly conflict.     Q8 Yes—the long-held tones.

Q9 It quickens the pace.     Q10 It shifts to 3 + 3 + 2.

Q11 It shifts abruptly.

Q12 It mostly coincides with the faster rate.

Q13 There are two levels of two-pulse metric groups between the slow pulse and the fast pulse:

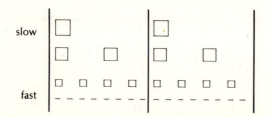

# 4

Example **4.1**

Q1    c.        Q2    a.

Example **4.2**

Q3    b.        Q4    Yes.        Q5        b.

Example **4.3**

Q6    c.        Q7    c.        Q8    c.

Example **4.4**

Q9    c.        Q10    In both statement and response.
Q11    Identical to the first.        Q12    Consistently in twos.

Example **4.5**

Q13    b.        Q14    a.

Examples **4.11–4.17**

Q15    4.11    O    (*Flute Ensemble of the Chief*)
        4.12    D    (*Mazurka*, Op. 33, No. 3, 1838)
        4.13    O    (*Paint It Sad*, 1971)
        4.14    D    (*Galliard*, c. 1529)
        4.15    O    (*Carmina Burana*, 1936)
        4.16    O    (*Narrative Song*)
        4.17    D    (*Orchestral Suite No. 3*, Gavotte 1, 1736)

Example **4.18**

Q16    When I am laid, am laid in earth.
Q17    Remember me, remember me.        Q18    11 times.

# 5

Example **5.3**

Q1    By wide leaps.        Q2    It generally covers a wide span.

Example **5.4**

Q3    Mid-range.        Q4    No.

Example **5.5**

Q5    From an already high level.

Q6    The beginning is low, the end high.

## Example 5.6

Q7    Mid-range.        Q8    Gradually.

## Example 5.7

Q9    By large leaps.

## Example 5.8

Q10   Very gradually.        Q11   In the third section.

## Example 5.10

Q12   Twice.

## Example 5.11

Q13   Two versions of the same melody.

## Example 5.12

Q14   Line 3.        Q15   The next-to-last line.

## Example 5.14

Q16   Second verse: "street" and "feet"; third verse: "frown" and "Brown."

Q17   It continues in the same way.

## Example 5.15

Q18   Verse 1: "There'll be some lovin' goin' on."
      Verse 2: "Gonna be some lovin' goin' on."

Q19   a) Two changes: on the second "little" and the third "little."
      b) Two changes: on the first "all" and the second "all."
      c) Four changes: on "had" and "farm," and on "ee" and "o" of the second "ee-i-o."

## Example 5.17

Q20   It stays the same.

## Example 5.26

Q21   Death's has the lower register; the Maiden's has the wider range.

Q22   "Ich bin noch jung."

Q23   The introduction is major, the conclusion is minor.

Q24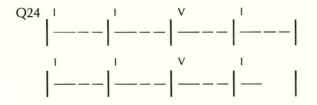

# 6

## Example 6.1

Q1    Variations in loudness.

## Example 6.2

Q2    The unison tenor line.

Q3    The necessity of concentrating on two independent lines.

## Example 6.5

Q4    The top part, because it has the principal melody.

## Example 6.7

Q5    During the unison section.

Q6    The unison section, because of the greater independence and activity of the two lines.

## Example 6.12

Q1    No. The accompaniment is independent of the voices.

## Example 6.13

Q8    The voice on the fast level, the harmonica on the slow, the drums on the fastest.

Q9    The fast level.        Q10    Both move to a slow level.

## Example 6.14

Q11    Yes.

## Example 6.17

Q12    The first pulse of each three-pulse group is silent in the Chopin.

Example **6.20**

    Q13   The tension level rises as voices are added.

Example **6.23**

    Q14   No.        Q15   It is less interesting.

    Q16   The role of the background is primarily rhythmic.

    Q17   The two clarinets compete with each other in imitation.

    Q18   Yes.       Q19   They mostly alternate.      Q20   Yes.

    Q21   Similar to.

# 7

Example **7.4**

    Q1   Yes.       Q2   They grow out of motives.

Example **7.5**

    Q3   They are equal in the first group, unequal in the second.

    Q4   The second group generates more tension, partly because of the irregular phrase lengths.

Example **7.6**

    Q5   Change of pitch level.      Q6   Much more elaborate.

Example **7.7**

    Q7   At the beginning; by a higher pitch level and more complex rhythm.

    Q8   Mostly in rhythm.      Q9   No, they are longer.

Example **7.8**

    Q10   "Light" and "God"; "night" and "God"; "day" and "day."

    Q11   The interlude cuts off before the melody is concluded.

Example **7.9**

    Q12   No, in neither section.

Example **7.10**

    Q13   The vocal ejaculations provide cadence-like punctuation.

## Example 7.17

Q14   The same.

Q15   They begin with material from (1) and (3), respectively, and then move on to the next section.

## Example 7.18

Q16   The continuation-transition is much longer than the presentation.

## Example 7.20

Q17  1 and 2.          Q18   3 and 4.          Q19   4.

Q20   2.          Q21   1, 2, and 5.          Q22   It moves higher.

# 8

## Example 8.1

Q1    Sustained sounds; whispers; the simple stepwise figure in each section; vocal outbursts.

## Example 8.2

Q2    Expanded.

## Example 8.3

Q3    "Two by two," "three by three," and "all alone."

Q4    The melody line descends at a rapid rate.

## Example 8.4

Q5    Slightly varied.

## Example 8.5

Q6    It changes to the major mode; all the others are in minor.

## Example 8.7

Q7    The performer changes the color of the harpsichord's sound.

## Example 8.8

Q8    Instead of returning to the original melody, the singer varies it greatly, starting at a higher pitch level.

Example **8.10**

    Q9   b.       Q10  b.       Q11  c.       Q12  a.

Example **8.12**

    Q13  No.       Q14  It plays part of the background chords.
    Q15  Rhythmic.     Q16  It attacks almost every pulse.
    Q17  Violin and cello.     Q18  Violin and piano.

Example **8.13**

    Q19  Its rhythm is changed.

Example **8.18**

    Q20  *c-b*.

Example **8.19**

    Q21  Tension is lowered at the beginning of A¹ by exact recurrence, then raised by variation.
    Q22  Having heard A¹ we expect variation, so tension is lowered; but beginning immediately provides a surprise, which raises tension slightly.

# 9

Example **9.1**

    Q1  It raises tension to a new level.

Example **9.2**

    Q2  Yes. Yes.     Q3  Longer—twice as long, in fact.
    Q4  It increases tension.

Example **9.3**

    Q5  It lowers tension, because of the repose of repetition.
    Q6  The variation raises tension.
    Q7  It provides a sense of completion and repose.

Example **9.4**

    Q8  The Dohnányi.
    Q9  The Dohnányi, because of greater variation and the interpolated passages before the opening phrase returns.
    Q10  Yes—changes in the harmony and the unexpected bassoon entrance during the last phrase.

## Example **9.5**

Q11 He makes the answering phrase ($a^1$) half again as long.

Q12 $a^3$ is longer still than $a^1$ and more complex in density.

Q13 The register is changed and more material is added to accompany the melody.

Q14 $a^7$ and $a^8$ are equal in length.

Q15 $a^4$.

## Example **9.10**

Q16 It comes as a surprise, its instrumentation is different, and its pitch doesn't "fit" the pitch relationships of the passage as a whole.

Q17 Gradual increase in loudness; length and increased activity.

Q18 Less, because its simplicity relieves the nervous energy built up in Section 2.

Q19 Repose through return to the kind of activity of Section 2; tension through added instruments.

Q20 Section 5, through an unexpected extension in relation to Section 3.

Q21 More repose, because of its comparative simplicity.

## Example **9.11**

Q22 Tension-increasers: the surprise of silence and uncertainty about its length; sudden loud sustained tone; sudden soft sustained tone; onset of flutter-tonguing. Tension-decreasers: repetition of similar sounds; soft sustained passage; quiet conclusion.

## Examples **9.12** and **9.13**

Q23 9.12.

Q24 More rhythmic energy, more variation.

Q25 9.13. The piano part is more complex, and the drums add momentum.

Q26 The melody suddenly drops out. In phrase $a^1$ of 9.13, tension drops because we've already heard that effect.

Q27 There is more variation, together with a higher pitch level, and more unexpected pitches.

# Index

Page numbers in italic indicate illustrations.

A
B 5
C 6
D 7
E 8
F 9
G 0
H 1
I 2
J 3